The I of the Storm for Teens
Finding Peace in the Midst of Conflict

The I of the Storm for Teens

Finding Peace in the Midst of Conflict

By Jane Simmons

Illustrations by Rebekah Ford

Published by **I Make the Difference Ministries**
www.imakethedifference.net

ISBN   1-59196-826-7

Library of Congress Control Number 2005902034

Printed in the USA by Instantpublisher.com

All Bible quotes are from the King James Version

Dedication

To the bright lights of my life:

My husband Gary, my partner in life and ministry, who lives and breathes these principles;

My son Keven, whose depth of understanding never ceases to amaze me;

And, my daughter Melodie, a teacher and a healer.

Acknowledgments

I would like to acknowledge my husband Gary for his endless patience and encouragement, as well as his ability to listen from the heart; Rebekah Ford whose wonderful cover design and illustrations help to tell the story; my colleague Reverend Duke Tufty for lovingly sharing the story "Don't Forget to Keep in Touch"; my friend and author Bobbie Kalman for her encouragement; my parents, Allan and Edith Chappell for holding the vision; my brothers and their families for their love and support; Anna Andes who assisted me in discovering ways this book might impact the young people for which it is written; my running buddy, Mia; and my good friend Reverend Priscilla Mercier, an inspiration and guide, as well as the Ministerial Class of 1999—on the heroic journey together.

Message to the Reader

I have found myself wishing I had learned these principles when I was a teenager. How different my life might have been had I found out then that I had the power within me to overcome the many problems I faced in those turbulent years.

The tools in this book can help you to deal with judgment and criticism in a positive way and find peace in the midst of conflict. Within you are all the answers you need to live a happy, successful life, no matter what may be happening around you. The "I" of the storm is a place of peace and understanding that you can always find when you turn to your heart.

Gandhi tells us that we must be the change we seek. As each one of us finds and expresses the love and peace that we are, we can be that change as we contribute to peace on earth.

May we all find that peace.

Jane Simmons
November 2004

Table of Contents

Forward

MANY YEARS AGO, I had a young student named Scott, who was testing for his first degree black belt in the martial art of tae kwon do. As the chief instructor, it was my custom to ask students to write a paragraph explaining what their black belt represented. Scott wrote, "Before I was a black belt, when I got into a fight I had to fight because I was afraid. Now that I am a black belt I can walk away."

What a profound realization this was for Scott to know the distinction between being in a threatening situation, and when afraid, having to fight. But being in the same threatening situation, and instead, being connected to inner feelings of confidence and well-being, which is what the black belt symbolizes, there is an entirely different way of being present to the scary situation. Scott could walk away because his strength and confidence came from within.

Thankfully, most of us won't have to face the threat of physical violence where there is little choice but to run, fight, or walk away, but each of us has bullies that keep us on edge in other ways. In those instances, it seems normal to run or fight when afraid or when someone or something seems against us. On the other hand, it may seem equally crazy to remain present to challenging situations in order to discover who we really are, when fear or defensiveness are no longer motivating factors. Can you imagine feeling so good about yourself and so centered in your own feelings of well-being and worth, that no person or situation could cause you to run or fight?

Often in my workshops and trainings I will ask the audience, "Where is the difficulty located in your life? Is it in the situation, or is the difficulty in how you're relating to the situation?"

Most people believe that the difficulty in their life is in the situations or people that appear against them. When this is the case, they are compelled to run or fight.

The spiritual approach, however, acknowledges that life's difficulty is located in how one relates to any given challenge. When someone or something appears to be against us, it is only possible because of how we are relating to the person or situation. When we relate from a place of wholeness and well-being, nothing in our experience can feel against us or diminishing.

The I of the Storm for Teens is about becoming like Scott, a peaceful warrior, a black belt in the art of being okay within oneself. Jane Simmons, a black belt in karate herself, has masterfully translated the principles of my book *The I of the Storm: Embracing Conflict Creating Peace* into an easy handbook for creating peace in the midst of any conflict. Jane has written this book especially for teens who struggle with issues of self-worth, fitting in, peer pressure, school bullies, and growing up in a troubled world.

She draws upon the rich spiritual traditions of the world's most respected religions from Christianity to Buddhism sharing relevant anecdotes and stories that warm the heart and enliven the soul. At the end of each chapter are helpful exercises that give the reader a practical experience in applying the spiritual principles of this book.

Jane's love for teaching and teenagers overflows onto each page. It becomes obvious to the reader that she is a gifted and inspired minister. Her ministry of empowering young people to know of their capacity to make THE difference and BE the difference that transforms the world, rings loud and clear.

Gary Simmons
October 2004

Introduction

IMAGINE, FOR ONE moment, that you came to this planet with a great purpose – of helping to create heaven on earth. Can you feel yourself volunteering for that great purpose?

Picture yourself being born into the perfect country, home and family in order to fulfill your divine destiny. See yourself committing to being a spiritual warrior, following the path of the hero's journey.

You have been given a certain set of gifts and talents that no one else has. You are unique, with a destiny that is divinely yours. Imagine for one moment that this could be the glorious truth about you, because .... guess what?

It is.

You are here to be God's ambassador on this planet, to be an expression of love, to be a stand for peace.......to make THE difference in your life and those around you. Sound like a challenge? This book is about how to do that.

CHAPTER 1

WHO HAVE YOU COME HERE TO BE?

"The river that flows in you also flows in me." Kabir

WHO HAVE YOU come here to be? What is it that you have come here to do? These are two very important questions to ask ourselves. The truth is that every single one of us came here to make the difference. Are you asking, "How can I make the difference? Does that mean that I have to do something earthshaking? Do I have to be famous or become an international leader? "

7

The answer is – no, you can make the difference right where you are. Look no farther than where you find yourself at this very moment. Your ability to make the difference in life is your divine inheritance.

In order to make the difference, we need to understand a few spiritual principles. In Unity, we teach that there is only One Presence and One Power in the universe and in my life – and that Presence is Good. It has many names – God, Father/Mother, Allah, Jehovah, Krishna, Great Spirit, the Divine, to list a few. All of these names describe the One Presence.

Try to imagine only Oneness. That means One Spirit, expressing as an infinite variety. If this is difficult to understand, picture an apple tree – one trunk, with lots of different branches and many apples, but with only one life moving through it. Every part of the tree is being nourished by the same roots. There is

nowhere that each branch ends and the tree begins. It is all one life.

In the same way, you and I are all attached to the same Source of Life. We are many branches and we all grow and "bear fruit" in our own way. It appears that we are separate, but like the apple tree, we are all nourished by the same roots – the Spirit within each of our hearts. Those roots connect us all.

If we look at God as the unifying energy that lies under all creation, it gets a little easier to see how we can all be part of a greater whole. The Buddhist poet, Thich Nhat Han points to the example of a blank sheet of paper. If we look at the paper, we actually see the sun and clouds that nourished the tree that became the paper. We see the logger who cut down the tree and the wheat that makes the bread to feed him or her. We see the grandparents of the logger, the activists who protest clear cutting forests, and so on. Our piece of paper contains the earth that the tree was grown in with all of its minerals and organisms. He calls this "interbeing". In other words, everything is inter-related and there cannot be any missing components. Every single one of us is a part of that whole and we have an important role to play.

In the book, The Sacred Balance, Canadian scientist and ecologist, Dr. David Suzuki wrote, "Every worldview describes a universe in which everything is connected with everything else. Stars, clouds, forests, oceans and human beings are interconnected components of a single system in which nothing can exist in isolation." We are truly One in the Spirit.

If there is only One Presence, and if that Presence is the life within you and me, then no one and nothing can be against any of us. Gary Simmons tells a story in his book, "The I of the Storm", of being counseled by a Hindu teacher who spoke these words to him: "No one is against you. You have no adversary in your life. There is nothing in the universe that is against you or your purpose...Make your path be about proving this truth and you will discover what wholeness really is."

Making your path be about proving this principle is called the hero's (and heroine's) journey, the way of the Spiritual Warrior. It is the sacred quest that enlightened masters have all made. Luckily they have blazed us a trail that we can follow, because it is a challenging path to navigate.

The first obstacle we encounter on the road to proving that no one and nothing is against us, is this question: if all is truly oneness, how is it possible that there is war and conflict? The world often feels like it is *very much* against us. People and situations can appear to be in the way of our desires and goals in life. How can it be true that there is nothing "out there" opposing us?

The reason it is so difficult to see that there is no one against us, stems from our belief that we are somehow separate from God, and that what happens outside of us can affect who we have come here to be. Instead of following our hearts, we have identified with our minds in a state of "spiritual amnesia". We have all temporarily forgotten our true identity – all branches from the same "Family Tree".

Just imagine, for a moment, if a branch on our apple tree decided it wanted to try and detach from the rest of the tree so it could strike out on its own! What would happen to it?

The branch needs to stay connected to its source of life. In the same way, we need to stay connected to our *awareness* of our oneness with God and each other so that we can be spiritually nourished. We do that in the heart, by realizing our true wholeness within. Since wholeness is the foundation of our being, then nothing can oppose us. Wholeness means just that – the whole. We can never be in opposition to another's spirit because Spirit is One, but when we lose our heart connection and forget our purpose, it can cause us to act out in fear. People can get hurt, the planet can be mistreated and countries can be at war.

Without an understanding of our divine heart connection, we *relate* to life much differently than if we know we are all one. When a situation looks and feels against us, it is really about *how we are relating* to that experience, rather than the experience itself. Do you see the difference?

It is time for us to remember the truth. When we do that, we claim our divine inheritance, our capacity to make the difference. We awaken from this dream of separation.

When Siddhartha Gautama reached enlightenment under the Bodhi tree after 45 days of contemplation in the Silence, he became known as the Buddha (which means the enlightened one). He was asked, "Are you a god?" He answered, "No". Then they asked him, "Are you a man?" Again, he replied, "No". So, puzzled, they questioned him once more, "If you are not a god and not a man, what are you?" He said, "I am awake".

The Buddha was not the only one to wake up. There have been many sages, mystics, masters and enlightened souls from many different cultures who have awakened. Their lives demonstrate and illustrate the hero's journey. If we follow the example of these wise beings, we can be awakened to our true identity and be guided to make the difference.

Jesus' life and teachings can give us some clues to follow on our journey to awakening. Let's look at some of His words: "But seek ye first the kingdom of God and his righteousness, and all these things shall be added unto you." (Matt. 6:33). The Kingdom is the Presence of God that is within every one of our hearts, and we are to seek it first. If we go within and find that place of peace, harmony and joy, we can feel God's Presence even during times of challenge, and be the one who makes the difference.

> *There is a Zen story told about a monk who was studying in the temple and happened to go to the marketplace one morning. He passed by a merchant who was selling fruit, and overheard a woman asking the fruit seller to give her his best apples. The merchant answered, "Every apple is the best one." And in that moment, it is said, the monk became enlightened.*

Every apple is the best one. Every one of us is here to make the difference, and we are the best one for the job we are here to do. Spirit 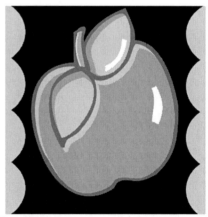 will provide us with all that we need. We just have to get still and listen to our hearts for the guidance that will show us the way on our journey.

Jesus also said, "He that believeth on me, the works that I do shall he do also; and greater works than these shall he do..." (John 14:12). The Man said *greater.*

We need to pay attention to that.

1. Who have you come here to be? To find out, make a list of the people you most admire and look to see what traits they have that you are drawn to. For instance, is it Mother Teresa's compassion, Gandhi's non-violent courage, your grandmother's gentleness, etc. You will be drawn to those people who mirror characteristics that are already within you. Make a list of those character traits and ask yourself, "Am I showing up expressing these things?" That is who you have come here to be.

2. Is there someone in your life that you have difficulty believing is "another branch of the Family Tree"? In what ways are you different from this person? In what ways are you the same?

3. Describe a time when you met someone and did not like them at first but as you got to know them, became good friends.

4. Read the story of the Buddha's awakening on page 12. Write about a time when you awoke from a nightmare. What happened in the dream? How did you feel while you were experiencing it? How did you feel when you woke up? Begin a nightly practice of journaling your dreams.

5. What do Jesus' words "Seek first the kingdom" mean to you? Where do we need to go to find the kingdom?

CHAPTER 2

AWAKENING TO OUR TRUE IDENTITY

"I wish I could show you, when you are lonely or in darkness, the Astonishing Light of your Being." Sufi poet, Hafiz

W̶HAT DOES IT MEAN to be awake? It means to become aware and conscious, to really see the truth. Our awakening is illustrated in the well known story of the Prodigal Son that Jesus tells in the book of Luke, Chapter 15. Here is a brief synopsis of the story:

> *There was once a very wealthy man with two sons who lived on a vast estate with many servants. One day, the younger son came to his father and requested his inheritance so that he could go and make his way in the world. His father gave him his share and*

the son journeyed to a "far country" where he squandered his money on "riotous living". Unfortunately, a famine came to the land and he found himself in

need. So he took a job feeding swine for a farmer. That was a particularly disgusting job for him, since he was Jewish. They considered swine to be unclean. He was starving and began to look with longing on the corn that the pigs were eating.

At this point, he "came to himself", having the realization that the pigs were eating better than he was, and that the servants

*who worked for his father were
well fed and cared for.*

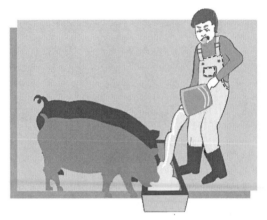

*He decided to return to his fa-
ther's house and ask to be hired
as one of his servants. The young
man returned home, but while he
was a long way off, his father saw
him coming and ran to meet him.*

*The young man said that he had
brought shame to the family and
did not deserve to be his son. But
the father welcomed him back
with open arms and prepared a
feast to celebrate his return.*

*The man's elder son heard all of
the commotion and came to see
what had happened. When he*

realized that his younger brother had returned and was being welcomed home, he became angry. After all, the elder brother had stayed and worked faithfully all this time and was never treated so royally.

The father told him that at any time he could have had his share as well. The elder son was deeply loved, and the man was rejoicing now because the younger son had been lost and was now found.

Jesus was a brilliant story teller. If we look at this story from the point of view that it illustrates our own journey, then it brings to every one of us a wonderfully inspiring message. No matter how far we may have strayed, we are always welcomed back into the arms of God. Our inheritance is the ability to make the difference, as we realize who we truly are.

When we squander that ability by misusing our gifts, we neglect our inner treasure. Then, like the story, a famine can arise in our lives. What would a spiritual famine look like? Imagine a time of feeling unfed, thirsting, wanting more. If you have ever felt unsatisfied and restless in your life, then you have experienced a spiritual famine. Why do we feel that dissatisfaction? The reason is because the outer world cannot give us what we truly seek, and to look outside of ourselves for satisfaction will lead us on an endless journey to nowhere! Remember Jesus' instruction to seek first the kingdom.

A "desire to acquire" in order to feel good about who we are, becomes a never ending quest that is doomed to bring us ultimate unhappiness. Roger Walsh, in the book Essential Spirituality says, "We keep hearing from advertisers, 'You can have it all'. What they don't tell us is that having it all is never enough."

Our search is not only with material possessions. Have you ever thought that your life would be better if you moved to a new school, a new town, a new job? This is known as a "geographical cure". Leaving our problems behind is never the solution because what happens is that those problems seem to follow us, showing up in new faces or situations, like a shadow that tags along behind.

We may also think, "If only I could lose 10 lbs. or find the right girlfriend or boyfriend, then I would be happy." And for a short time, we can be! Ask anyone who has lost weight or fallen in love. At first, life is wonderful, isn't it? But then our habitual patterns reassert themselves, the old issues creep back and we realize that there is no such thing as "happily ever after" when it comes to living life from the outside in. In the words of "Jennifer Unlimited", "Every time I close the door on reality, it comes in through the windows." The problems just keep showing up, no matter how we try to escape them.

Looking only to the outer world for our happiness, we set ourselves up for what I like to call a "swine experience", which is the realization that we are not doing what we came here to do. We wake up one day and see that "this isn't it", we have strayed off the path. Then we "come to ourselves", as the son did, and return to our true home, which is the spiritual awareness that is within our own hearts. When we do, what happens? Spirit welcomes us back with open arms, overjoyed to have us awaken to our true nature. That which we are seeking is seeking us and God's love for us is unconditional, eternal and welcoming.

This is a story about a son's travels, but the truth is that we don't actually have to "go" anywhere to find our answers. Home is right where we are. By returning to the home within our hearts, we can awaken to the truth of who we are and realize that the Divine Presence has never left us. Spirit has been there all along, just awaiting our recognition. *This is where true lasting happiness can be found!*

Interestingly, the Buddha tells a similar parable, the difference being that the son is a prince and as a small child, wanders out of the palace walls and gets lost. He forgets he is a prince, and lives as a pauper until his father rescues him and reveals his true identity.

These parables have the same underlying message – *we are divine beings who have forgotten the truth.* Imagine for a moment that a king wanted to find out how it felt to be a poor person in his kingdom. He could dress in rags, sit outside the palace walls with a begging bowl, but in the back of his mind, he would know that come nightfall, his nice warm bed in the castle was awaiting him. If he truly wanted to ex-perience how it felt to be destitute, he would have to forget he was royalty. In the same way, in order for us to truly experience living in the physical world as human beings, we have to temporarily forget that we are spiritual beings living in a body.

How do we get back into the conscious realization of who we are? Our remembrance comes by looking inside of our hearts instead of being distracted and mesmerized by the outside world. The true treasure lies within. It is our wholeness. Our problems in life arise when we become disconnected from our wholeness and sense of self worth, thinking that life is better "out there".

Unity's wonderful poet, James Dillet Freeman tells the story of a young boy who looked through the plain windows in his home every morning and noticed that the windows in all the houses on the other side of the valley were glowing as if they were gold. One day, he goes across the valley and when he gets there, he discovers that the windows in those houses are as plain and ordinary as the windows of his own house. However, as he looks back at his home, he is astonished to find that the windows there are glowing as if they are gold.

The gold is right in our own backyard!

1. Describe a time when you have acted as the younger prodigal son in your family. Have you ever felt like the elder brother in the story?

2. Think of a television commercial that gives the message that you are not complete unless you use the product being promoted.

3. Identify some of the ways you look outside yourself to feel good – for example, it might be through excessive eating, shopping or playing video games. What are the drawbacks to using these kinds of activities to find happiness?

4. How would you show up differently in the world if you really knew your wholeness, if you knew without a doubt that you had within you all that you needed to be successful?

CHAPTER 3

THE I OF THE STORM

"Close your eyes......and awaken" Anon

THE GOLD THAT IS BURIED in our own backyard is the "I" of the storm. At the center of the hurricane is the "eye". This is a place which is calm and peaceful, no matter how much destruction the storm may be wielding. We can use this illustration to describe our own lives. Sometimes, it feels like storms are all around us; problems at school, divorce, health issues – whatever it may be, there can be turmoil in our lives. But at the center, at the "I" there is only peace. Our job is to find that center and remain at peace no matter what is happening outside of us. The following story, told by Catherine Marshall in the book, "Stories for the Heart" illustrates that peace.

> *There was once a king who offered a prize to the artist who could paint the best picture of peace. There were many entries*

to the contest. The king looked
at all the pictures, but there were
only two he really liked and he
had to choose between them.

One was a picture of a calm lake.
The lake was a perfect mirror,
with peaceful towering mountains all around it. Overhead was
a blue sky with fluffy white
clouds. All who saw this picture
thought that it was a perfect illustration of peace.

The other picture had mountains
too. But these were rugged and
bare, with foaming waterfalls
tumbling down. Above was an
angry sky, filled with heavy rains

and flashing lightening. This pic-
ture did not look peaceful at all.

But when the king looked, he
saw behind the waterfall, a tiny
bush growing in the crack in the
rock. On the bush, a mother bird
had built her nest. There, in the
midst of the rush of angry water,
sat the mother bird on her nest
..... perfect peace.

Which picture do you think won the prize? The king chose the second picture, ex-plaining that peace does not mean being in a place where there is no noise, trouble or tur-moil. It means being in the midst of all those things and still feeling the serenity that is al-ways in your heart. That is the real meaning of peace. At the center of the storm, there is still-ness.

Turmoil isn't a new feeling. It's been around for awhile. In the book of Mark, Jesus fell asleep on a ship with the disciples and a great storm arose. The disciples became very anxious and woke Him up in great fear. Jesus awakened and what does He say? "PEACE, BE

STILL" (Mark 4:39). With the speaking of those words, the storm subsides.

What a wonderful metaphor for the storms of our lives. We may sometimes feel that we are being bounced about by every wave, at the mercy of the ocean of life. When that happens, we can go within to the Christ that "lies sleeping" and ask for help in calming the storms. On the ocean's surface, there may be tremendous storms but at its depths, there is only silence, calmness and peace. In the same way, at our depths, in the stillness of our hearts we are always at peace. No matter what is happening, we can stay centered in the "I" of the storm. Even when we experience conflict in our relationships with others, we can go below to that place of peace. That is our spiritual wholeness.

"The dove of peace has first to find a resting place for its feet in our hearts, before it can make its home in our surroundings...." says N. Sri Ram, in the book, Thoughts for Aspirants. When we find peace within, we will bring that peace to our world.

THE DIVINE GIFT OF THE HEART

The Buddhist nun, Pema Chodron says in "Start Where You Are", "We are one blink of an eye away from being fully awake." That's pretty close! We don't have to travel far, but we do need a good map so we know where to look. How do we access our Divine Essence? Where can we find the I of the storm? Where do we dig for the gold? There is an ancient Hindu fable that illustrates where to look.

The gods were having a meeting. The purpose of their meeting was to discuss where to hide humanity's power. They were afraid it would be abused if it were too easily found. So they came up with some ideas.

"Let's hide it on the highest mountain", suggested one of the gods. They all agreed. Then they realized that eventually humanity would climb the highest mountain and find it there. So they thought again.

"I know", said one god excitedly, "let's hide it in the deepest ocean!" Again, they saw that humanity would one day go to

the depths of the sea and find it there.

They thought some more and said, "How about the deepest forest?" The answer was the same -- eventually they would visit the forest and find it.

Finally the answer came forth. "The one place they will never look, the one place where it will be safe is..... WITHIN THEIR OWN HEARTS! They will never think of looking there!"

And so since that day, the legend goes, the divine essence has been hidden within each of our hearts. It is the I of the Storm. We all have hearts of gold.

So the truth is that wholeness is not outside of you, nor is it separate from you. There is nothing you have to add to yourself in order to be whole. It is the essence of your true nature and spiritual identity. Is wholeness something that can be here today and gone tomorrow? No, if you are whole now, you are always whole. Unity's second principle tells us that we are each a Divine Spark of the One Presence and One Power. That is true wholeness and is our most prized possession. Because wholeness is the essence of who we are, nothing can oppose us. *But we must stay centered in our hearts in order to find that wholeness.*

Don't be fooled by how simple this is – staying focused in your heart is a powerful way of being. It may be simple, but is it easy? As in our fable, the great power of the Higher Self is right within us, closer than our very breath. Like the Tin Man in the Wizard of Oz, we have had it all along. We can choose to go directly to the heart or take a trip to Oz and back before discovering what was always there.

Until we follow the path with heart, we will never be satisfied. Jean Shonoda Bolen said, "If you choose a path with heart, it may be difficult, but there is joy along this path and as you travel, you grow and become one with it." On the other hand, she adds, "If you choose a path out of fear, anxiety travels with you and no matter how much power, prestige and possession you acquire, you will be diminished by it".

But here's the thing: we can't use our heart power if we don't take the time to get still and feel the love within us. If you study a map of Florida, even memorize all the cities, you still haven't visited it until you actually go there. Reading about Disney World and being

there are two very different experiences. In the same way, if you just read about the power of the heart and don't practice connecting with it, you haven't really experienced "Space Mountain" within you.

Unity's fourth principle is that we have tools that help us to access the Divine Spark within us. Prayer and meditation are two of those tools. Heart centered prayer is the way to connect with the Power that resides in each one of us. The heart, as our center, is where harmony and balance occur. And I have good news! We all have one!

The heart contains the key for us to open the door and access Spirit. Seeking that wholeness is actually seeking the kingdom, as Jesus taught. Every time we use our heart energy to transform, we bless the world. We also bless our own bodies. Loving from the heart creates a coherence that aligns all of our internal systems so that our body begins operating in harmony. Feeling love is how we connect to our Higher Intelligence and experience the Presence of God.

When we know our own wholeness, then we are truly free. This is the peace that Jesus speaks of, calling it "My peace" in John 14:27. We need to look within our hearts to find the wholeness that is eternally there, no matter what happens outside of ourselves. We carry it with us wherever we are.

Mother Teresa is quoted in the book, The Intelligent Heart by David McArthur, as saying, "Prayer enlarges the heart until it is capable of containing the gift that God makes of Himself". When we "enlarge the heart" through prayer and increase our capacity to love, then life becomes a heart trip instead of a head trip. And it is just a blink away.

AWARE-APY QUESTIONS TO PONDER

1. What is one storm you have experienced in your life?

2. How did you handle it?

3. What were the consequences of your actions?

4. Did you find any peace in the midst of the situation?

5. Imagine what the storm might become when you relate to it from your heart instead of your head.

CHAPTER 4

AGREE WITH THINE ADVER-SARY QUICKLY

"Wherever you look, there is the face of God." The Koran

A knight returned to his castle at nightfall. He was a terrible mess

– his armor was dented, his helmet had fallen to one side, and his body was covered in mud and bruises. The lord of the castle

met him at the gate and asked
"What has befallen you, Sir
Knight?"

He replied, "Sire, I have been la-
boring in your service, robbing
and burning and pillaging your
enemies to the west."

"What?" asked the startled no-
bleman, "But I haven't got any
enemies to the west."

"Oh..." said the knight, after a
pause, "well, I think you do
now."

Whoops. Making enemies can happen
for many reasons. Unmaking them is what this
chapter is about.

Everything in existence has a center. My
center and your center, found within our
hearts, can never oppose each other, because
that is where we truly connect. When separate
heart cells are placed together, at first they beat
at different rhythms. And then one by one,
they begin joining one another in harmony until they are all beating in one accord. Hearts
never battle, only heads do.

The mind is very helpful when doing what it is intended to do – for instance, comparing, analyzing, sorting and processing information. We get into trouble, however, when we let the head do what it is *not* designed to do – lead us. The heart is supposed to be the leader, with the head as a very capable second in command. When we shift to the heart, we feel the oneness of our divine connection and experience the Presence within. This gives us access to deeper understanding and wisdom. By moving our attention to the Presence of God, we can allow Spirit to guide and direct our actions, no matter what is happening in our lives. That is the "I of the storm". We experience the "I" by feeling love.

Feeling love toward someone extends our energy field. Consciously choosing to open our hearts, we stay connected to our partner. On the other hand, when we close our hearts, we contract that energy field. This reinforces our sense of separation. Have you ever walked into a room where moments before, there has been an argument? Without being present while the harsh words were spoken, could you feel the anger in the room? The expression, "you could have cut the tension with a knife" describes that kind of a situation. When someone's energy field contracts, we can feel it.

By moving to our center and extending our energy field, we can rediscover the principle "there is no one and nothing against me." To get a clear understanding of this principle, it is important for us to really see how life is mirrored back to us from every person and situation we meet.

There was once a man who guarded the gates of the city walls and one day a traveler came to the gates to enter. He asked the gatekeeper what kinds of people were found within the city.

"What were the people like in the last city you visited?" asked the gatekeeper.

The man answered, "They were terrible, hateful people. They were always complaining and treating me with disrespect."

The gatekeeper told the man, "You will find the same kinds of people here." And so the man

*decided not to enter the city and
he moved on.*

*A little while later, another man
came to the city gates and asked
the same question. The gatekeeper, once again, asked him
what kinds of people were in his
previous city.*

*This time, the traveler answered,
"They were wonderful! So loving
and kind! They treated me like
royalty."*

*The gatekeeper wisely answered,
"You will find the same kinds of
people here."*

Those around us mirror what is inside of us and mirrors can only reveal  how we are showing up.

"Agree with thine adversary quickly."
These are words spoken by Jesus in the book of

Matthew 5:25. What exactly do they mean? They don't mean that we go along with someone who may be hurting us. Agree, in this case, means to work things out.

When we feel threatened and become defensive, we can use our own feelings of fear as evidence that someone is against us. We do this to manage the discomfort. Let's face it, conflict is uncomfortable. That is why we project our fears onto others. If someone else is to blame, then we don't have to look inside ourselves for the problem. *And yet, if we take responsibility and seek the answer within, we can find out what is missing in order for us to experience our true wholeness.* That is the real meaning of agreeing with our adversary. Invariably, whenever I have applied this principle, I have found that what has been missing is my connection to my own sense of self worth. Had I been connected, whatever was said or done wouldn't have had the effect on me that it did.

You know you are in relationship to an "enemy" when your first inclination is to be in control of the situation, or to be right and make the other person wrong.

What arises as an adversary in our lives, then, comes from within us. "The enemy" is the belief that there is someone or something against us. This could be our body, an illness or physical condition.

We could look at divorce or an unsympathetic friend as the enemy. Whatever seems to be against us we see as the adversary. Remember, the enemy is a reflection of our belief, it is not the truth. We have to relate differently  to the situation in order to dismantle this untrue belief.

It is important to see this and know how we are creating resistance and tension in our lives. What we fear and believe becomes our experience, bringing with it the appearance that someone or something is against us. If we take responsibility for our fear based actions, we can stay in a place of peace, knowing our wholeness. *So, embracing that which appears as the enemy is the formula for healing.* Jesus understood the power of this truth and that is why He taught it. Agree with thine adversary quickly.

The famed Swiss psychologist, Carl Jung said, "Everything that irritates us about others can lead us to an understanding of ourselves". Think about those words for a moment. Could it be that people you are at odds with are actually showing you a part of yourself that is keeping you from knowing who you really are? If someone can "push your buttons", that is a great way to pinpoint an area that is in need of some healing. By becoming conscious that those around us can point to our "sore spots", we can use our relationships with each other as a way of healing. When we recognize that we mirror for each other what is inside of us, we can now take steps to heal, since we learn to look within rather than outside for the answers.

> *There was once a sailor who was never seen without a smoking cigar hanging out of the side of his mouth. He had a parrot that developed a very bad cough and worried, the sailor took the bird to the vet to find out what was wrong with his beloved pet.*

> *The vet listened to the parrot and then turned to the sailor and*

said, "There is nothing wrong with this parrot, he is imitating you!"

Those around us can point the way to our own healing.

So, in the presence of an adversary, if we can shift our attention within, knowing that something is being mirrored for us, we can move to our center and become peaceful and then take authentic action.

Jesus told the disciples in the Sermon on the Mount that anyone could love those who love in return. In Matt. 5:46, He said "For if ye love them which love you, what reward have ye?" As a child of the Most High, we have been commissioned to love where it is the most difficult to love. Each one of us is called to take the higher road. We are here to make the difference. We do that by being "who we came here to be."

Treat your enemy as you would your most beloved friend if you are to claim your true wholeness and worth. Of course, this doesn't mean that you allow another to abuse you. **It is never ok for someone to hurt you.** If you are in an abusive situation, tell someone you trust – for example your parents, your teacher, your minister or doctor. It is important if you are in any kind of danger to be safe.

We are not talking about life threatening situations, here. We are talking about the many fears that aren't true, the ones that live "rent free" in our heads and cause our lives to be unhappy – the "paper cuts" in life. When we take authentic action and relate to life from a place of willingness to make the difference, that willingness becomes our amazing SUPER POWER. Move over, Spidey…. Loving others is our true natural state and it is the key required to "enter the kingdom".

Hey, no one said being a Spiritual Warrior was easy. It requires strength, courage, willingness and stamina. Think of Luke Skywalker and his arduous training with the Jedi master, Yoda, in order to face and overcome his greatest enemy, Darth Vader. Using "The Force" of love and acceptance, he was able to free both himself and his father from enslavement to the "dark side". We can think of Jesus as our Master Trainer. He may not be green or three feet tall, but like Yoda, Jesus' teachings can help us to turn our enemies into loving friends. How can we do it? His wisdom provides us with a wonderful formula that can have amazing results.

Jesus taught in the book of Matthew, a four step method to wholeness that looks like this: "**Love** your enemies; **bless** those that curse you, **do good** to them that hate you and **pray** for them that despitefully use you and persecute you." This is advanced Jedi training and these are the Peacemaker's Tools.

What does our mind say about all of this? It has difficulty wrapping itself around these teachings. It thinks thoughts like, "Pray for those who persecute you? What's up with that?" The mind cannot conceive of it. *But the heart can.*

Yes, it is a rather tall order, but it is what we are called to do. It is our glorious purpose on the path of the hero's journey. We achieve it through the power within our hearts. Jesus didn't teach about the power of love just so we could send each other Valentine's cards. He taught it because he knew it was the *formula for transformation.* He understood the amazing power of "The Force" to change lives. We all have the Force within us. We just need to bring it forth. So let's look at how we can do that by following what I like to call the "Four Floor Formula". (Try saying that quickly ten times).

Love means to accept, embrace, and value. In the presence of the "enemy", think of the person or situation as a mirror for you, showing you that place where you are not connected to your wholeness. If you *were* connected, as Jesus was, you could not feel intimidated or threatened. Do you see that? This is an important point to really get. The question to ask is this: what is the missing resource that would help me to stay connected to who I really am? Is it self confidence? Is it a feeling of knowing your own worth? The answer you get from asking these questions is very valuable information. This person or situation is actually *for* you, not *against* you, since it is showing you what is missing in your capacity to relate from your wholeness. By embracing and valuing this person or situation, you are able to grow in awareness and understanding. "Love your enemies" does not necessarily mean you will like what is happening or that it magically be comes "nice". *It means accepting and valuing the person or situation for mirroring for us where we are not connected to who we really are.*

Unity's co-founder, Myrtle Fillmore literally loved her body back to health. She had tuberculosis, a terminal illness and a condition that was considered a death sentence at that time. Told by doctors to get her affairs in order, Myrtle knew that if her health deteriorated any more, she didn't have long to live.

She attended a lecture where she heard the words, "I am a child of God and therefore do not inherit sickness", Myrtle took those words to heart and spent all of her time in prayer, loving her body, blessing every cell with wholeness. She asked each cell for forgiveness for ever believing it was anything less than perfect. It took two years, but by embracing and loving "the enemy", her health was restored.

This is the first floor in our process. We have to be willing to accept what is happening in our life. The irony is that by accepting and loving something as it is, we now can access the power to change it. A nurturing environment of love and acceptance provides the right conditions for growth. That is true for plants, animals and children. It is also true of our own minds and bodies. We must remain connected to the experience like a wire is connected to a light. The "switch" is our willingness to be present.

Now, let's move up to the second floor. To **bless** means to endow something or someone with the capacity to be a positive force in your life. In other words, look for the good in the situation or person. Do you remember Joseph in the book of Genesis, whose brothers sold him into slavery? Now that was sibling rivalry! At the end of the story, despite all that had happened to him, he was able to say to his brothers, "Ye thought evil against me, but God meant it unto good..." (Gen. 50:20). In the same way, you and I can look at whatever is happening in our lives and find the blessing by knowing that God meant it for good. We can look for and find "God's fingerprints" all over the situation!

Knowing that our enemy is simply a mirror to that place within us where we are not aware of our connection to God, then by blessing our enemy, we reclaim our power. By looking for the good in the situation, we actually create the opportunity to find the blessing. And it is all about attitude.

There was once a farmer who had a horse. One day, the horse escaped from the corral and was

*gone. His neighbors came over to
tell him how sorry they were that
his horse was missing. He simply
said, "Maybe".*

*The next day, the horse returned
with two other wild horses and
now the farmer had three.*

*Two days later, the farmer's son
was trying to ride one of the wild
horses and was thrown to the
ground, breaking his leg. The
neighbors rushed over to com-
miserate with him and the farmer
answered, "Maybe".*

*A week later, the army came
through town, conscripting all
the able bodied men into service
for battle. Because his son had a
broken leg,
he was
passed by.*

When things
happen to us that
appear to be bad,
with the right atti-

tude, we can find the blessing. When we are willing to embrace a situation as a gift, we can see what inner resource has been missing and bring it forth. Knowing that there is some good in it, creates the opportunity to find that good. This is the second step of our "Four Floor Formula".

We move up to the third floor as we take authentic action. To "**do good**" means doing the right thing. To be honest, probably the last thing we want to do when someone treats us badly is to do good. Instead, we may feel the need to defend ourselves or to strike out. This is the time when we need to remember "there is only One Presence and One Power" and "there is no one and nothing against me".

Doing good means letting go of needing to be right and instead, focusing attention on who you have come here to be. If I need to be right, that means someone has to be wrong. If I can, instead, shift to "doing the right thing", take ownership for my part in the situation, and take responsibility for my actions, then I can be blessed by the circumstances. I become the "Way of God" as Jesus taught and then something happens in that situation that can *only* be done through me. In each situation, I am either the way of God or *in* the way of God and there is no in between.

We may have very good reasons why the other person is wrong. We may believe we have been victimized and attacked. Again, abusive behavior is not acceptable. Violent actions are never to be condoned. Doing the right thing does not mean being a doormat. *Jesus was anything but a doormat!* Sometimes doing the right thing means leaving a situation that is hurtful and not allowing that person or situation to do any more harm. However, needing to be right, or seeking revenge can come at the expense of our spiritual growth. We never lose by doing the right thing. That is because when we do, we are in complete alignment with our true nature as spiritual beings.

There was once a man who had a disagreement with his brother. They were neighbors and had a dispute about a stream that bordered the property line. The arguing grew so intense that finally, they stopped talking to one another altogether and as time went by, the wedge between them grew wider and wider.

Finally, the elder brother decided to build a tall fence so that they

*couldn't even see each other. He
thought that as long as there was
an invisible wall between them,
he might as well create a real one.
So he hired a traveling carpenter
who was visiting his town. After
instructing him on how to build
the fence, the brother left to go
on vacation while it was being
constructed.*

*Upon his return, he saw his
younger brother coming to greet
him. Expecting a fight, he prepared to defend himself. To his
amazement, the brother had tears
in his eyes and embraced the
elder brother, asking for his forgiveness. The younger brother
said "What you have done is such
a symbol of forgiveness that I feel
so ashamed of my past behavior.
Please forgive me." And he wept.*

*The elder brother was puzzled
but remained silent until he
reached his home. There, instead
of the fence he had ordered,
stood a beautiful bridge linking*

the two properties. The elder brother was immediately ashamed as well and asked the younger brother for his forgiveness. Their reunion was joyous.

The carpenter was asked to remain in the town and continue to bless the people with his good will. But he replied that he needed to move on, there were other bridges that needed building.

Are there fences that need dismantling in your life? Building a bridge is "being the Way of God". We have reached the third floor and we are heading for the top.

The top floor, the "Upper Room" in our hearts is where we go to **pray**. Praying means talking to God or giving our thoughts to God.

It helps us to remain aware of God's Presence. Praying for our enemies is a way to shift our attention to our center, our spiritual identity, the place of true power. When we pray, we lift the situation up into the peace of the "I".

Praying for our enemies does not mean asking that it goes away! It means asking your heart to show you the truth. The purpose of being in the "I of the storm" is *not* to make the storm go away. It is for holding the space for the power of love to do its work.

As a young adult, my brother had an experience with the power of prayer. He was out at a restaurant with a group of his friends one night in the bitter cold of winter and was wearing a brand new warm coat that was barely a week old. Putting the coat on the back of his chair, he left the area for a few minutes and when he returned, the coat was gone! Someone had stolen it. He had to make his way home that night without a coat in subzero temperatures.

My family was angry. A brand new coat! Leaving him to freeze! But my brother chose to pray about it and by centering himself in his heart, was able to remain calm and compassionate. In fact, he prayed for the person who took the coat and then released it into God's hands. Imagine our surprise as two days later, the coat was returned to him in perfect condition. That day, I learned a real lesson about the power of sincere and loving prayer.

When Jesus was on the cross, He gave the ultimate forgiveness prayer. "Father, forgive them; for they know not what they do." (Luke 23:34) No one ever lived up to their own words better. It was a prayer that gave Him freedom from judgment, and demonstrated to those who persecuted Him that they had no power to act against Him. This prayer shifted Jesus to His center and allowed Him to act from His place of wholeness. From this powerful prayer, He was freed and resurrected.

If we pray for our enemies, we also shift our attention to our spiritual center, where we can experience oneness with God and oneness with those who appear separate from us. We are not *victims but victors* and prayer helps us to realign with the power of God that resides in our hearts. It has been said that the best way to get even is to forget.

Relearning ways of responding to the world takes time. Be patient with yourself. But remember, like our Way Shower, Jesus, we can be freed from any situation that has challenged us and then be resurrected into a new, more powerful understanding of who we are. By following this formula for success, we can dismantle any situation that appears to be against us and find the good that is awaiting us. May the Force be with you.

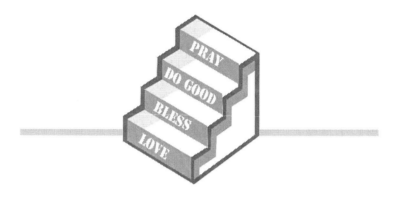

AWARE-APY QUESTIONS TO PONDER

1. What "enemies" do you have? Divide a piece of paper into three columns entitled "Body", "People" and "Life Situations". List under each column any things that you may be having problems with in your life.

2. Choose one item from your list and apply the "Four Floor Formula" to it. Journal the following questions: How is this showing me where I am not connected to my wholeness? How can this be *for* me instead of against me? What positive action can I take to come to a place of peace?

3. Spend time in prayer, asking Spirit for guidance on healing this "adversary".

4. What happens when you "love", "bless", "do good" and "pray" for that person or situation?

5. Repeat this formula for each and every "enemy" on your list.

CHAPTER 5

TWO STREAMS FLOWING TOGETHER

"It is difficult to make a man miserable while he feels worthy himself and claims kindred to the great God who made him." Abraham Lincoln

THE FOUR WINDS OF CONFLICT

"...conflict with another person can simply be a string around your finger to remind you of your own spiritual work." Karen Alexander

STORMS JUST DON'T HAPPEN by accident. A hurricane needs certain conditions in order to rise up, such as temperature, wind velocity and humidity. In the same way, certain conditions in our lives can cause storms of conflict to arise. These conditions are what Gary Simmons calls the "four winds of conflict": separation (not understanding the oneness behind all of creation), misperception (seeing life through our own beliefs), competition (thinking there is not enough to go around) and defensiveness, (fear of what may be "out there" that can harm us).

The four winds of conflict have their roots in listening to the head instead of the heart. However, and this is the key, because you are a spiritual being and know your wholeness, you can direct your attention to the "I of the Storm", your heart, and through the characteristics of wholeness, bring forth change and transformation.

These characteristics are the "antidotes" that can be applied to the four winds of conflict. They are:

o for separation - communion (the experience of oneness that can be found in the heart)
o for misperception - principle (seeing truthfully with the eyes of the heart)
o for competition - purpose (being the one who can bring peace to a situation)
o for defensiveness - the power of non-resistance (going with the flow). Let's look more closely at each of these conditions and see how we can use them to discover how to make the difference.

SEPARATION

If we are really whole and complete, why don't we know it and feel it? It can all be linked to our beliefs.

From the book, "Tuesdays with Morrie", there is a story about a small wave that is bobbing along happily in the ocean. Suddenly he notices that the waves in front of him are crashing against the shore. Becoming very fearful, he cries out and tries to warn the others by yelling, "Look out, we are going to crash!"

Another wave calms him down and says, "Relax, you are safe. You're not just a wave. You are part of the whole ocean."

Can a wave ever be separate from the ocean? No – and in the same way, you and I can never be separate from the Presence of God. We are born knowing only oneness, with an unconscious innocence. In fact, as a baby, we cannot tell the difference between "you out there" and "me in here". Life is all one. There is no separation. What happens to that experience of oneness as we grow up? We discover that life does not always go the way we think it should and because of that, throughout our childhood, we make some faulty decisions about ourselves and forget we are more than just a single, isolated wave. Here is the important thing to remember: It is not what happened to us as children, that causes the problem. It is the *decision* we made about ourselves *because* of what happened, that can get in our way.

Those decisions become beliefs that we

 want to keep hidden from those around us. We cover up the mistaken beliefs by wearing a mask to the world. In psychological terms, it is called our "persona". It is what we believe to be the

acceptable part of ourselves that we show to others. The parts we think are unacceptable don't go away, however. They just go underground. They may become repressed, but those childish mistaken beliefs remain. Maybe we cover them up, but they are still there, hidden and buried, known as "the shadow". We create emotional barriers in order to protect ourselves.

For instance, suppose you have accepted the belief "I am not good enough". You may wear a mask to the world that appears as if you are confident and happy, but underneath, the worry of not measuring up will be affecting you in ways that you don't even recognize. Eating disorders or substance abuse can very often be attributed to these faulty beliefs. That is what can happen when we keep things underground.

It is like holding an inflated beach ball under water. It takes lots of energy to keep it down and eventually, no matter how long you hold

it under the water, that ball is going to slip and pop up somewhere. Our "internal beach balls" do much the same thing, seemingly appearing out of nowhere to ambush us.

Like a hidden stowaway on a ship, these beliefs are taking an "illegal" free ride. These hidden parts are a creation of the head, not the heart – and when they cause us to act out, we are showing up in life as "who we are not" rather than "who we came here to be". They will continue to cause us problems until we become aware of them and bring them out into the light. Those around us who are "pushing our buttons" can help us to do that.

Carl Jung said, "That which we do not confront in ourselves we will meet as fate". In other words, what we try to hide from *inside* of ourselves will show up *outside* of us in some form. We set up a sort of "virtual reality" made up of our own fears.

Here's the thing: Other people can mirror for us what we are hiding within ourselves. We will find that we are attracted to people who mirror the positive traits within us and *we will avoid those who mirror parts that we find unacceptable or unlovable*. This is called projection and it can cause us to feel like someone or something is against us. When I project, I "make you the matter with me" because it feels less painful to look outside of myself for the problem and blame someone else, than it is to look within and see something that I may be afraid to find.

Most of us were not given messages as we grew up that we were children of God. We were born into a world that was unable to mirror the truth for us. Consequently, it is difficult to grow into adolescence with our sense of wholeness intact. This causes a false sense of separation. That is why we can feel threatened, limited or unsafe. In order to manage those feelings of separation, we learn coping behaviors such as needing to be right, controlling or avoidance. However, these behaviors keep us stuck in "who we are not".

What beliefs do you have that are making you feel small and unworthy? Here's the good news: we can always make a new choice. We can transform any experience by choosing to see it differently. Every moment, we can choose how to direct our attention. Instead of listening to what the mind tells us, we can go to our heart and see it from Spirit's perspective. We can look differently at our experience and reframe what we see, remembering who we really are. Who are we really? The Sufi creation story tells it like this:

In the beginning of Time, the Creator wanted to behold the beauty of Creation and so a mirror was fashioned. As the mirror was held up to the Creator's face, says the legend, so great was the light and the power and the beauty of the image, that the mirror shattered into billions of bright shiny pieces of every size and shape and color and description. Thus were the people of the world created: reflections of Spirit and all unique facets of the One.

We are reflections of One Spirit, all wearing various costumes. So whenever you find yourself lost in feelings of unworthiness, ask your heart these questions, "How can this be possible if we are all reflections of the One? What is the Truth about this?" The Truth is that there is only One Presence and One Power, that you are a spark of that Divine Presence and that you are a powerful being who creates your experiences by the thoughts you choose to think. Knowing this, instead of separation, you can make a new choice and experience your oneness through communion.

COMMUNION

Communion means being connected to life. It also means "common union". Communion is the "I of the storm" of separation.

The first step of wholeness is seeing the distinction between you and your experiences. Look at your hands – you have hands, but you are not your hands. In the same way, you have experiences but you are not your experiences. You have thoughts but you are not your thoughts. It is important to understand this distinction, because any thoughts of unworthiness are just that – thoughts – they are not who you are.

When we confuse our thoughts and experiences with who we are, instead of seeing them as things that we have, we can feel unsafe and insecure. If we judge our self worth based on what is happening to us, we are looking for wholeness in the wrong place. When we are not connected to who we have come here to be, then when someone judges us, we will react by trying to *disprove the accusation* and miss the opportunity to create communion.

Have you ever been judged by someone? How did it feel? I want to let you in on a very great secret, one that can help you overcome judgments whenever they arise. The secret is this: *A judgment is never about you.* It may be about what you said or did. It may be about what the other person needs. It may be about what is missing for them in your relationship. But it is never about you. In fact, it is *for* you, since through it, you can discover where you are not connected to your sense of self worth.

For instance, if someone came up to me and said, "Jane you are a frog", I would have little or no reaction, except for perhaps wondering what planet the person is from. I *know* I am not a frog. It would not affect my self esteem whatsoever and would simply pass through me like a breeze through a screen door. If, however, they said, "Jane, you are a lousy minister", WO! Chances are very good that I would have a *much* different reaction, triggered by my own secret fears around my ability as a minister. Forget the screen this time. I might be tempted to "catch" the second statement.

If I catch it, then it *is* about me. Why? Because it is something for me to look at! The good news is that we can become aware of our healing needs as we watch our reactions to judgment. If I get defensive when someone criticizes me, it is a wonderful opportunity to discover the faulty belief that is still underground. What valuable information that is! If I choose to see every person who judges me as my teacher and ask "What is it you are here to show me?", then that teaching will be revealed to me and the healing can happen. Judgment is the package, but we have to be willing to unwrap it in order to receive the gift. The gift is awareness and growth. So if we don't buy into those judgments, but instead recognize that "it is not about me", then we have wonderful opportunities to become the connecting link between God and the situation.

For example, if I realize that "you are a lousy minister" *really* means that there is something missing for that person and is not the truth about me, then I can listen from the heart

and get to what is the real issue. Instead of taking it personally, I can participate in a healing process by really hearing the other person.

How do we do that? When someone criticizes or judges us, we can use three powerful words, "TELL ME MORE".

When someone lashes out at us, it is rarely about what they have originally said. By embracing their words and asking to hear more, we unravel the real meaning. After the person has elaborated on the issue, next come the questions, "What do you need?" or "What is missing for you?" This "tell me more" way of relating is the magic formula to help us deal with judgment in a healing way.

I used these words when I had a conversation with a member of my former congregation who was upset that I was leaving the church to get married. The conversation began with some very sharp, angry words directed at me. I was momentarily taken aback, but then remembered to use the magic phrase, "tell me more". With each sentence, the truth was slowly revealed that he was feeling a lot of sadness and pain. My heart opened with compassion as I really listened. After receiving the gift of being heard, he was able to begin letting go.

If I had answered the first exchange with anger, outrage or defensiveness, it would have stopped the process. By realizing that his criticism was not about me and using the words, "tell me more", the result was that we were able to come to a place of love and healing.

These words can unlock a judgmental situation and help us to find the gift at the center of it.

"Tell me more" does not mean that we never get a chance to say how *we* feel about the situation. After we have sincerely heard what the other person has to say, then we can share. By saying, "Now that I have heard you and you feel understood, may I share what is missing for me?" This is non-violent communication and speaking from the heart is the gateway to true healing.

LISTENING 101
"Listening is the shortest distance between two people."
Anon

How are your listening skills? Do you really hear someone when they talk to you or do you wait for them to finish so that you can say what is on your mind. If you do not have the capacity to be changed by what is being said to you, then you are not really listening. This doesn't mean that you have to agree with it, but be willing to change how you are relating so that a connection is established. "Tell me more" keeps the lines of connection open. True listening from the heart creates communion.

The Chinese verb for listening consists of three characters. Each character is made up of an image: one is 'heart and ear', one is 'paying attention' and one is 'two streams flowing together'. These images depict empathy (heart and ear), becoming fully present (paying attention) for the purpose of creating communion (two streams flowing together).

When we really listen from the heart, we can become two streams flowing together and experience true communion. Feeling connected to life, we can build bridges and be the connecting link between God and the person or situation. We can be who we've come here to be.

AWARE-APY QUESTIONS TO PONDER

1. Describe a time when someone judged you. How did it feel?

2. Imagine that the person was actually a teacher for you and that the judgment was *for* you. What could it be telling you about false beliefs you may have hidden within you?

3. Try using "tell me more" the next time someone lashes out at you with a judgment or criticism. Journal what happens.

4. Make a list of both inner and outer re-sources you have, to use in a time of conflict. Examples of inner resources might be strength, compassion, cour-age. Example of outer resources could

be friends, brothers or sisters, librar-
ies, school counselor, etc.

CHAPTER 6

YOU IN THE VIEW

"The true person sees what the eye sees and does not add to it something that is not there." Chang Tzu

MISPERCEPTION

O KAY, SO if there is only oneness, how is it that enemies and adversaries are created? How can there be an enemy when the entire universe is conspiring is bring us good? The reason is that we all see life through the influence of our own personal sets of judgments and perceptions. We give our life meaning through the things we believe. In other words, I participate in creating my own experience, because *I make my life mean what it means.* The way we choose to relate to our experience actually helps to dictate what our experience becomes.

There was a man who was driving along a winding mountain road. Another car suddenly came around the bend and the

*man who was driving it stuck
his head out of the window and
as he passed the first car, yelled
"PIG!"*

*The first man was taken aback
and became very angry at his ex-
treme rudeness. As he shouted
back, "JERK!" he rounded the
bend and saw a pig in the middle
of the road.*

MEANING MAKING

So what are you making your life mean? It can be very revealing to ponder that question. For example, when you look into your wallet and see a $10.00 bill, how prosperous do you feel? It isn't the money that decides what it means. It is the value that you give to it that determines if it is enough. If you are on your way out to shop at a dollar store, it may be plenty for what you need to buy. If you are taking a friend out to dinner, the $10.00 will have a much different meaning to it.

Unity's third principle says that we create our world through our thinking. What we routinely think about and believe becomes our experience. Sometimes, we believe that we are human beings trying to be spiritual, when, in fact, the truth is that we are *spiritual beings having a human experience*, just as Jesus did. As spiritual beings, we have the power to change our lives through our deeply held thoughts and beliefs. If you want to change your world, change your thinking.

Life doesn't happen *to* us but *through* us. Our thoughts and feelings create mental and emotional states that influence how we respond to what is happening. As I heard Rev. Dr. Johnnie Coleman speak at a seminar once, "I am the *thinker* who *thinks* the thought that becomes the *thing*." Our predominant patterns of thought set the stage for us to experience "the world as I see it".

We project onto events and circumstances their meaning and relevance. If we are in a traffic jam and there is no hurry to get to where we are going, it is less of a hassle than if we are late for an important appointment. Our experience of those two traffic tie ups will be markedly different.

"You in the view" means that we filter our experience through our personal beliefs and assumptions, using "evidence" that we gather to prove that what we see is the truth. This is no more than a viewpoint and the irony of this is that our misperception actually blocks us from seeing what is really true!

Robert Alter writes, "If we only knew everything everybody has been through in their lives, our judgment of anybody, even the most bizarre person muttering curses to us as we pass him on the sidewalk, would come to a screeching halt." The following story told by Stephen Covey illustrates what he is talking about.

There was a man riding in the subway who had his three very young children with him. The children all looked to be under the age of 5 and the man was just letting them run wild. They were causing a lot of trouble in the subway car and finally, Stephen felt compelled to get up and speak to him.

He approached him and asked rather curtly, "Excuse me, will you please control your chil-dren?" The man looked up with a start as if he was just awakening and apologized profusely. Then he explained.

*"I am just on my way home from
the hospital. Their mother died
this morning and I don't know
what I am going to do." His voice
trailed off and Stephen felt his
heart open to him.*

His perception of the situation had
changed radically.

We bring our meaning making to every
situation we encounter. Life arises as neutral,
but it can become positive or negative depending on how we view it. Imagine a group of
people all standing in a circle facing the inside,
with a center point. Every person in that circle
would see the center from their viewing point.
Which one would have the "right" view? Everyone would!

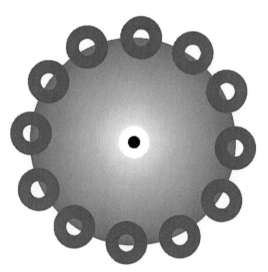

The thing to remember is that our "viewing point" can actually cover up how things really are. For example, imagine a young basketball star in high school being described to you by his girlfriend. Now imagine hearing about him by his greatest rival on the basketball court. And next, imagine his description by his basketball coach. How about by his dentist?

Each person would talk about this young man from his or her point of view and could give a totally different description, depending on what their attention allowed them to notice. The simple act of recognizing how we distort reality through our perceptions can help us to move to a place of power.

It is essential for us to see this. If we don't see that the meanings we attribute to what happens to us actually shape that experience, we can remain in a "victim role" in which we feel powerless to change. The problem we encounter can be changed, but we need to widen our understanding in order to make that change. Einstein said "The significant problems we have cannot be solved at the same level of thinking with which we caused them." Taking the higher road means changing that level of thinking.

When we are stuck in "meaning making", we will fill in the gaps – that is, whatever it is that we don't know, we will fill in with what we believe. When we do that, we can make assumptions based on our past experience. For example, if someone close to us appears to be upset, we may automatically assume it is because of something we did, even though it may have nothing to do with us at all. That is why young children living in a household that experiences divorce, can believe that it is something that they did that caused it to happen. Is this the truth? No, but in that child's experience, it will be. Virtual reality.

Have you ever decided that something was true and then built a whole scenario around it? Decided what you were going to say and do? And probably what they were going to say and do? And then after all that, found out that what you imagined was not at all the way it really was? When we don't have all the answers, we fill in the missing pieces with what we believe. The worst part is that we may act on those beliefs, faulty or not! Becoming aware of how we are "looking" at our lives, through the filter of our beliefs, is the first step in freeing ourselves and living from our wholeness.

So, if we are unhappy with what is happening in our outer world, where do we have to go to change it? Within ourselves. Imagine you are watching a slide show. There is a projector that casts the image of the slide onto a screen. Suddenly a picture is showing that you don't like. Would you walk up to the screen and try to change the picture there? No you would simply change the slide.

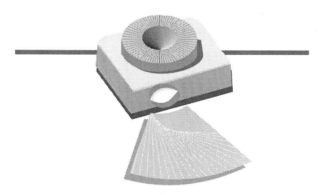

Our thoughts work the same way. If we don't like what we are seeing on the outside, we need to change the inner slide. When we use our challenges to find a new way of seeing, we can grow beyond the limited perception we may have about ourselves.

A large two-engine train was crossing the country. After it had gone some distance, one of the engines broke down.

"No problem," the engineer thought and carried on at half power. Farther on down the line, the other engine broke down and the train came to a standstill.

The engineer decided he should inform the passengers about why the train had stopped, and made the following announce-ment, "Ladies and gentlemen, I have some good news and some bad news. The bad news is that both engines have failed and we will be stuck here for some time." He could hear the sound of rising angry voices.

Then he added, "The good news is that you are not in an airplane." The angry voices melted into laughter. It suddenly changed everyone's perception.

It all depends on your point of view.

When I trained in the martial arts, we spoke aloud a statement before each class. These are words attributed to Mahatma Gandhi:

I will keep my thoughts positive because my thoughts become my words.

I will keep my words positive because my words become my actions.

I will keep my actions positive because my actions become my values.

I will keep my values positive because my values become my destiny.

Thoughts become my destiny, as I make my life mean what it means.

PRINCIPLE

"What the caterpillar calls the end of the world the master calls a butterfly" Richard Bach

There was once a young man named Joshua who decided to leave his home and family. Josh began living on the streets and even talked some of his friends into leaving their homes and their jobs to join him. They roamed together as a gang with only the clothes on their back and started hanging out with the wrong crowd. Sound like trouble? What advice would you give our gang leader, Josh and his friends? How might we judge their way of life? If you are curious about what became of them, you can read all about it in the New Testament. You might recognize Joshua better by the Greek spelling of His name......Jesus.

Do you see how the mind tells us things that are not necessarily true? Is there a way to measure what it is that we believe, and decide if it is really the truth? We do that by returning to principle. The second characteristic of wholeness is principle. Principle means seeing life as God sees it. It is the "I of the storm" of misperception.

Principles are laws, they don't change. They give us a solid foundation from which to view our lives. Therefore we can hold any perception up to the light of principle and see if it measures up.

If we are seeing an adversary, then that *alone* is evidence that we are not seeing it right. Why? Because the principle tells us that there is only One Presence and One Power! No one and nothing is against me! So, if our human perception is telling us otherwise, we can know it is faulty and then instead of giving our power to our judgments, we can call on principle. It can be our measuring stick.

Our beliefs about life will dictate how we see things. If what we are seeing disagrees with principle, then it isn't true. When we  come from principle, we come from peace, because we learn that we may not be able to change what has happened to us, but we *can* change how we view it and what we carry with us because of it.

So, how do we use principle to "see it right"? We need to look with the heart. Love sees oneness. Love connects us to all of life. When we don't see our oneness, fear and distrust arise, but we can move to the "I of the storm" of misperception as we see with the heart. In the Buddhist tradition, there is a teaching that says we need to place the fearful mind in the cradle of loving kindness. The heart is that cradle and from this new perspective of love, we can ask ourselves, "How can I see this differently?"

You might call it "same place, different heart" – seeing with the eyes of Spirit. We do that by looking within our hearts and allowing Spirit to guide us and show us the Truth. Through heart-centered vision, we have the power to shift our perception and pronounce it good, because now something else is at the wheel – love.

Remembering that life is a mirror for us, it takes a shift in looking at the outer situation that will change our perception. We can ask ourselves this question: "Is what I am seeing based on principle?" Or "How is it possible that if there is only One Presence, I am feeling antagonistic toward him or her?" Even though it may appear that we are separate when we look with our human eyes, we can apply principle and go within our hearts for the truth. The heart knows.

Imelda Shanklin, from the book, "What Are You?" asks the question, "Can God create a two-year-old tree in a second?" The answer is, "Yes, but with our vision, it will take us two years to see it!"

By seeing with our "spiritual eyes", we widen our perspective. *Principle means seeing life as it really is.* You and I have a choice, moment by moment, in how we view the things that happen to us.

There is an ancient story told of a Sufi trickster named Nasrudin. One day he happened upon a man who was crying. When he asked him what was the matter, the man showed him a small bag and said, "Everything I own is in this little bag. I am so poor!" And he wailed on.

Nasrudin grabbed the bag and ran with it until he was out of sight. Then he set the bag down in plain view, knowing that the man was headed in his direction and hid behind a rock.

When the man discovered the bag, he shouted for joy, thanking God for its return. At this point, Nasrudin sprang up from behind the rock and asked the man, "How is it that this bag once made you weep, and now makes you jump for joy?"

An instant can change not only our perspective, but our feelings as well.

So, when we find ourselves reacting defensively, we can ask ourselves, "What am I making this mean". Then we can measure it against principle and see that *what we are making it mean is the real adversary!* The mirror can only reveal how we are showing up.

This does not mean that we discount our experiences or feelings. It means that we include the heart in our interpretations of challenging situations. In order to heal false beliefs, we need to take our attention off of the mind and go instead to our center, the heart. It takes courage to show up in life knowing that nothing and no one is against us. The word "courage" comes from the French word, "coeur", which means "heart". Following heart principles, we can walk the hero's path with faith. By seeing it right, we can unlock any door that blocks our freedom and transform our world.

Phil. 4:8 says, "Finally, brethren, whatsoever things are true, whatsoever things are noble, whatsoever things are just, whatsoever things are pure, whatsoever things are lovely, whatsoever things are of good report, if there be any virtue and if there be any praise, think on these things." These beautiful words of wisdom from Paul are the key to transformation. This is another tool from Unity's fourth principle – affirmations. By speaking positive words of truth and affirmation, we begin the process of seeing those truths come to pass in the outer world.

1. Take a moment to get still and quiet your mind. Imagine breathing into your heart and as you do, focus on someone that you love and appreciate. It could be a good friend, a child, or a pet. Let feelings of appreciation fill your heart and as you continue feeling love, choose a situation in which you have a challenge with another person. Continue breathing into the heart and as you do, now send the feelings of love to the person you have a challenge with, and ask your heart for help in guiding your actions in the situation. What does Spirit guide you to do?

2. Write your thoughts and feelings around this statement: "If there is no one and nothing against me, and I am seeing this person as against me, then I must be seeing this wrong". What am I making this mean? How might I see it differently?

3. Name a time when you made a judgment about something and found out later it was not

correct. How was your assumption based on the past?

4. For the next week, commit to looking at everything that happens to you with "new eyes". Examine how each situation can be for you, and ask to be shown how you can see it differently.

CHAPTER 7

MISSION POSSIBLE

"The world needs dreamers and the world needs doers, but above all the world needs dreamers that do." Sarah Ban Breathnack

COMPETITION

WHAT HAPPENS WHEN we compete with others in life? Someone has to lose. Competition can result when we don't get what we need and we think there's "not enough for me". How do you feel when you lose in a relationship? Angry? Resentful? The purpose of relationship is to love and support one another. How sad it is when relationships become battle grounds.

The need to be right or control can arise when we are in competition. Conflict exposes our "tender spots" and needing to be right comes from trying to protect those tender spots and find comfort in the discomfort.

No one likes to feel like they are wearing a big "L" for Loser on their forehead. Sometimes in the embarrassment of being caught making a mistake, we can become defensive and blame someone else or insist we are not wrong. If our self worth depends on always "looking good", then we will resort to these defense strategies to avoid the pain of being laughed at. Have you ever felt the need to be right or to make someone else wrong in order to save face? I read the true story, published in the London Times, of a man from England named Neil who needed to do just that.

Neil discovered an owl nesting in his backyard. He began to go outside each night and hoot to the owl. To his delight, he would hear a hoot in reply. Night after night, Neil continued his hooting and even kept a log of his conversations with the owl.

Then one day, Neil's wife started talking about this with her neighbor who said that her husband, whose name was Fred, had also been going out every night to hoot to the owl. At this point,

the two women realized that
their husbands had, in fact, spent
an entire year hooting at each
other. The owl wasn't even in-
volved at all!

The funny part of this story is
that even when the two men discovered their mistake, they continued to do it. They refused to
admit that they had been mistaken. Night after night, they
continued hooting away, knowing all the while that the voice
hooting back was not the owl.

Imagine knowing that something isn't working and yet still doing it! Have you ever done that? This is a classic story of needing to be right. Who wins?

So the question to ask is, "Who do you have to be in order to *need* to be right?" You have to be insecure, fearful or inadequate. However, those things are not the truth about you. You may *have* fears and insecurities, but they are not who you are. Do you see the difference? The truth is that if you need to compete in order to get your needs met, you are not showing up connected to your own sense of wholeness and self worth. Needing to be right is a symptom of acting out of "who we are not" and is a way of trying to prove our self worth by masking feelings of low self esteem. When we lose our heart connection, we forget that we are all one.

Look at the example of our Family Tree. Would two branches in that tree ever compete with one another? No, because each branch is connected to the oneness that it is. We discover that same connectedness when we love from our hearts. The heart is the mechanism through which we discover the truth that we are all one and there is no need to compete. There is no lack in the universe, only abundance. There is more than enough for all of us to go around!

There is a big difference between being in competition and overcoming obstacles. Our soul, (the "I"), moves us forward and that movement can lead toward challenges in life. Rising above those challenges helps us to grow and stretch in ways that separate us from "who we are not". So, not competing does not mean that we may not have to sometimes struggle in order to rise above adversity in our lives. Part of the process of growing into who we have come here to be, entails overcoming challenges on our path.

Think about the difference between overcoming challenges as opposed to competing with a sense of "there's not enough for me". Which one helps to identify and develop our inner source of strength? Which one points the way to the truth that there is only oneness? A good question to consider is this: "Is my behavior being motivated right now by fear or by love?" If I am coming from my head, worried that there isn't enough for me, chances are pretty good that I am being motivated by fear. If, however, I sink down into my heart and sincerely ask for guidance, I will always be shown how to rise above the storm. I will be given the direction needed to be who I have come here to be, which is my purpose. The heart is the doorway to that purpose.

There is a delightful story told about a group of nine contestants competing at the Seattle Special Olympics. They were assembled at the starting line for the 100 yard dash. When the starting gun went off, they all began running with excitement, all except for one boy who stumbled on the asphalt and fell. He began to cry.

The other eight heard him crying and they all slowed down and looked back. Every one of them ran back to him. One girl with Down's syndrome bent over, kissed him and said "That will make it better". Then all nine linked arms and walked together to the finish line. Everyone in the stadium stood and the cheering went on for 10 minutes. They were all winners.

FINISH LINE

PURPOSE

The third characteristic of wholeness is purpose. Purpose is the "I of the storm" of competition. *Purpose is the universe's intention, through each one of us, to be the Presence of God.* Our purpose is to love, to be the avenue through which God expresses on the earth, to be the Christ unto our world. Jesus was the Christ of His world. You are the Christ of your world. In others words, we are how God gets around! If we are living from anything less than that, conflict will arise from within us from expressing "who we are not" instead of "who we came here to be".

So our worthiness is not mirrored by outer standards, but by our ability to be the avenue for God's expression. When we truly know our worth, we will make the difference that we came here to make.

Sound like a tall order? Luckily the entire universe supports us in being who we came here to be! Our Creator encoded our purpose deep within us at the cellular level. We arrived on earth with all we needed in order to make the difference. However, the problem arises when we forget our true identity and find ourselves overwhelmed by the things that are happening around us.

If we confuse our experience with who we are, and if we make that the basis of our self worth, then what happens when we have negative experiences? We are at the mercy of them. If we let our relationships, for example, determine our worthiness, then what happens when the relationship ends? If we let our job define who we are, then what do we experience when the job is no longer there? Who are we really?

If we feel that we are "not enough", nothing outside of us can complete or fulfill us. Our wholeness is our most valuable possession. It is our divine inheritance and true identity. Searching our hearts will help us to find the real treasure that eternally lies within each one of us.

In my life as a minister, I was the leader of a church of 150 people for four years. When I left that position to be married and begin writing, I had a period of time where I had to remember that my job did not define who I really was at the center of my Being. It was a period of great growth for me and I was able to overcome the feelings of loss that rose up. ("Who am I without my congregation? ....without my family and friends? ....without my paycheck?").

It took a great deal of faith to step out of the role that I was very accustomed to and start something brand new. The conflict that I felt eventually led me to remember that I am not my experience. It also led me to uncover some feelings of insecurity and fear that I was able to embrace. Through that experience, I have grown as a minister into more than I could have previously imagined.

Our heart will guide us in directions that help us to uncover who we have come here to be. We can use our heart as a compass to help us on our quest to discovering and living our purpose.

In the Gospel of Thomas, it is written, "If you bring forth that which is within you, what you bring forth will save you. If you do not bring forth that which is within you, what you do not bring forth will curse you." Our purpose is to bring forth our unique gifts to bless the world. If we "hide our light under a bushel", the result will be what is known as "divine discontent". Until we take complete ownership of our purpose, to be the Christ of

God in our world, we will not find inner peace or wholeness. "Our world" can be anything from our bodies, our families, our communities, to our planet. Bringing the Christ into every situation that we find ourselves is the reason we are here. We are each here to take care of our little corner of the earth and make the difference right where we are.

> *I read the story about a real estate agent who was going through the countryside and came upon an absolutely gorgeous farm. So he stopped to chat with the farmer and said, "You have a magnificent farm, one of the prettiest I have ever seen. God has really done a great thing here."*
>
> *The farmer thought for a minute and answered, "Yeah, well you should have seen it when God had it all alone."*

We are here to be the hands of God in action!

Conflict and adversity are the spiritual "midwives" that help us to clue in to this truth.

Like any birth, it does not come without struggle! After the labor, however, something new is born. As we choose to be the way of God, no matter what the seeming difficulties, we help to change the world.

The television program, "Joan of Arcadia" is about a teenage girl who sees and talks to God. The instructions she is given usually don't make sense to her, but always end up blessing someone in her life. The Supreme Being shows up in many different guises from spiked and tongue pierced Goth-like teenagers to kindly grandmotherly types. In fact, one day Joan asks God, in exasperation, "Is every day, like.... Halloween to you?" She isn't far wrong. Everyone who shows up on our path is the Divine in disguise. Deepak Chopra calls it "Spirit, playing hide and seek".

If we treat each other as "God in costume", then our job is simply to listen, as Joan does, to the guidance we receive and act on it. In the midst of conflict with others, Spirit beckons us to become more. We are invited to show up in life, and to be present. It is only then that we can break through limited thinking and create miracles! Like the farmer taking care of the garden, God needs our hands to bless those around us and make positive changes here on earth.

Every challenge is an opportunity to shift your attention and awareness to the questions, "What is my purpose in this situation?", "Who am I really?" and "Who have I come here to be?" By asking these questions, you can discover that you have been brought into the kind of situation that needs *your* energy, *your* vision, *your* understanding of principle.

Jesus is our role model, our Way Shower, and He demonstrated the Truth that with God, all things are possible. He said, "I am the way, the truth and the life." (John 14:6) All of us are here on "Temporary Assignment" in order to be the way, the truth and the life. Making the difference is our spiritual job description. It is our "Mission Possible".

You are either the way of God or *in* the way of God. Being the way of God means to bring the love in your heart into every situation. Whenever we are allowing Spirit's love to move through us, we are being the way of God. If, however, we are being blaming, judgmental, unforgiving, unkind or fearful, we are being *in the way* of God.

When we see God in every situation, we are being the truth of God. When we hold all of our experiences to the light of principle, and consult our heart, we can see that Spirit is at work in each situation. Jesus saw the truth. He did not let the outer circumstances stop Him from His healing ministry. No matter what was in front of Him, He saw it rightly, looking with His heart.

What does it look like to be the life of God? When we are open, willing, flexible, affirming and supportive, we are radiating the life of God in all that we are and do. Staying in the awareness that we are the life of God, we can be a positive force for good. So the question to ask ourselves in each situation is, "How can I be an agent for God right here and right now?" Each of us has the ability to let our light shine and bless the world as the following story illustrates.

There was once a rabbi who was approached by his students with a complaint about the evil that

*was everywhere in the world.
They were intent upon driving
out the forces of darkness. The
students requested that the rabbi
counsel them and so he suggested
that they take brooms and attempt to sweep the darkness out
of the cellar.*

*The bewildered disciples applied
themselves, using all their vigor-
ous energy to sweep the darkness
out of the cellar, but to no avail.*

*The rabbi then advised his fol-
lowers to take big sticks and vig-
orously beat at the darkness to
drive out the evil. When this also
failed, he counseled them to go
down again into the cellar and to*

*protest against the darkness by
lighting a candle.*

*When they lit and shared their
lights, the darkness had been
driven out. "It is better", said the
rabbi, "to light a candle than to
curse the darkness."*

We share the light and live our purpose
through our hearts. We are being the **way** of
God, when we love with the heart. We are being the **truth** of God when we look with the
heart, and we are being the **life** of God when
we lead with the heart. *Love, look and lead with
the heart and we make the difference.*

LOVE   LOOK   LEAD

AWARE-APY QUESTIONS TO PONDER

1. Describe a situation where you "needed to be right" and made the other person wrong. Did it resolve the problem? Was there a win-win solution that you could have found?

2. Have you ever lost in a competition? How did it feel?

3. Make a list of things you have, as opposed to who you are. Include in your list, thoughts, beliefs, feelings. Do you see how you are not those things, but you have those things?

4. Describe a time when you were "in the way" of God. What action might you have taken in that situation to instead become "the way of God"?

5. Consult with your heart and ask the question "What is my purpose?" Write in your journal whatever comes to mind, without judging any of it. Keep writing

for a minimum of 5 minutes without stopping. What does your heart tell you?

CHAPTER 8

DON'T FORGET TO KEEP IN TOUCH

"The purpose of life is a life of purpose." Robert Byrne

THERE IS A WONDERFUL story, written by Rev. Duke Tufty, which illustrates our journey on earth, shows our capacity to make the difference and demonstrates the way that we can make that happen.

> *Once upon a time, you and I existed as Spirited Souls in another dimension, a dimension which is really quite different from the way it is here on earth. At that time and in that place, we heard exciting, marvelous stories about a journey that could be taken – that journey called "life on earth". It was filled with so many experiences that the great-*

est desire we had, was to go on that journey.

So we went to God and made a request to go. God said, "Are you sure you want to go? Life on earth is very different from your experience here. In this place, all we know is the Light of Truth, but on earth, because it isn't finished, because it is still engaged in the creative process, it is sometimes easy to get confused. People there often wander into the darkness and they experience trouble because of that. Are you sure you want to go?"

As eager, Spirited Souls, we responded with an enthusiastic "Yes, we don't care if the earth isn't finished; we want to be part of that creative process. We want to go more than anything else!"

God said, "There are no guarantees as to how long your journey will last. Life on earth might be two days, two years, twenty years, seventy or more."

As eager, Spirited Souls residing in the Light of Truth, we understood that our existence is eternal. It doesn't begin or end with life on earth. We understood that regardless how brief the journey, we would engage in magical, mystical and rewarding experiences that would live on in our memories forever. We also understood that if and when we chose, then at another point in time, there would be another journey with new experiences.

So we quickly agreed and said, "Yes, God, we accept those conditions. We want to go. The amount of time our journey lasts makes no difference."

And God said, "The vehicle that would allow you to go on this journey through life is called a body. There are no two alike. Your body will be unique to you and you alone, and it will provide you with many wonderful, different experiences. But there are no guarantees as to what kind of body you will have. It might be big, it might be small, it might be strong, or it might be frail. It might be extraordinarily different from any other body that you may see."

*As eager, Spirited Souls, we re-
sponded with excitement and
enthusiasm about the prospect of
receiving our very own special
body. We promised to love and
care for it. We assured God that
we would be proud of it. In the
Light of Truth, we understood
that a body is a great gift. It is a
treasure, an incredible blessing.
We understood that the differ-
ences and variations of one's
body are a result of the miracu-
lous, creative power of God. In
the Light of Truth, we understood that our body is a magnifi-
cent temple in which the soul
will reside. So we persisted in
our request to experience life on
earth.*

*God said, "Are you sure you want
to go? Earth is a place that is far
from being finished. In many
ways, it is still in its infancy.
There are no guarantees in re-
gards to the experiences that will
come your way. You may experience bigotry or discrimination.*

You might be subject to harsh criticism and prejudices. There are those who have wandered into the darkness and they may reject you and consider you less than equal."

As eager, Spirited Souls, residing in the Light of Truth, we wanted to be part of a movement that takes humanity closer to the re- alization that every person is an object of praise. We wanted to be part of that order that brings the Light of Truth to earth. We wanted to establish a sense of oneness, unity and harmony on earth. So we said, "Yes, God, we want to go."

And God said, "There are no guarantees. If you are born into an environment that is unloving, you may become emotionally in- jured. You may experience lone- liness and pain. You may lose sight of your specialness. You may even become unloving your- self. On this journey, you may

become confused. You may wan-
der into the darkness and lose
your way, where you will lose
sight of the journey's value."

But as Spirited Souls, residing in
the Light of Truth, we under-
stood that the journey is a pro-
gressive one. We understood
that every experience will pro-
vide for us something of great
benefit. We understood that life
on earth is a learning process in
which every individual, as well as

humanity as a whole, is moving into the Light of Unity and Love. We understood that every experience on the journey has purpose and meaning. So, as eager Spirited Souls, we persisted in our desire to go.

And God said, "OK, you can go. You will be allowed the great privilege of taking the journey called 'life on earth'. But the journey is not without purpose. Your mission will be to express the Light of Truth so that the darkness can be dispelled. On this journey, you will have the benefit of many experiences. Don't fear them, for every experience has meaning and purpose, even if you don't recognize it at first. Don't resist or fear the experiences of life, but rather embrace them. By turning to your heart and embracing those experiences, you can receive the gift within them."

"Using the power of Love, you can be the Light that shines in the darkness. You can be the one that brings kindness, goodness and compassion to places where there is none. You can make the difference. Trust your heart. It is your compass and will make your journey a peaceful one. Your heart will keep you from getting lost."

As eager, Spirited Souls, we were willing to go on this journey but we were confused and so we asked God, "How will we know

how to use our wisdom, our com-
passion? How can we make the
difference?"

And God answered, "All you
have to do is go to your heart and
ask and I will give you all the
guidance you need." So as we
were being directed out the
heavenly door, God's final words
were, "This is where your journey
begins and this is where your
journey will end. For when you
arrive back at this point, you will
be greater in every way. Have
confidence in yourself. There is
nothing to fear. You have every-
thing you need to complete this
journey in a peaceful way."

So, as we embarked upon our
journey and began to move away,
God called out, "One last thing,
my precious child, don't forget to
keep in touch."

So here we are, you and I, on this journey,
this marvelous, exciting journey called "life on
earth". Some of us have just arrived. Some of

us have been here for a long time, but here we are together, making this journey. We are like little children caught up in the excitement of going out to camp for the first time, who forgot all the things their parents told them to do. At times, each of us can get caught up in the sometimes chaotic and confusing excitement of life on earth and forget why we are here. We forget the purpose of our journey.

The truth is that we are Light Bearers. We are God's ambassadors to the earth. We are here in the right time and the right place, to bring Light to the darkness. We are here to discover and use the power of Love and express God's goodness. We can embark on this journey and go through it in a peaceful way. We can be in harmony with all that is. We have been given that power and we carry it with us everywhere we go, inside of ourselves. We simply have to remember to keep in touch and we do that in the heart.

You are needed for this job! You have just enough time to do that which you came here to do. There is no time to waste. *So don't forget to keep in touch.*

AWARE-APY QUESTIONS TO PONDER

1. To get the most out of this wonderful tale, find some soft, meditation music and play it. Ask a friend to read the story out loud to you while you get still and quiet and listen with your heart. How does the truth of it resonate with you?

2. Imagine that life on earth was an earned privilege and that our time here was limited. How differently would you spend your time than you do now?

3. Is there a situation where you can make the difference, and bring compassion where there is none?

4. Spend time each day (at least 20 minutes), breathing into your heart and feeling love and appreciation. Use these times to keep in touch with God, by asking for guidance. Keep a journal of your experiences.

CHAPTER 9

THE PATHWAY TO PEACE
"What we resist, persists." Unknown.

DEFENSIVENESS

KEEPING IN TOUCH with God is so important, because when we don't feel connected, we can become defensive. We feel the need to defend ourselves and put up barriers when we believe we are separate. Some of our childhood experiences taught us that it can hurt to be connected, dependent and innocent. In order to manage those feelings of separation, we have learned different coping strategies, such as needing to be right, as we saw in Chapter 7. Other ways we try to cope with conflict are needing to control, avoidance or resistance.

Have you ever had "control issues"? Needing to have things be a certain way actually shuts down the creative process. Quantum physics tells us that at any given moment, infinite possibilities are present. However, as soon as we insist something has to be a certain way, then that field of possibilities collapses. There may be many paths open to us, but the instant we decide "This is the only way it can be", all the others vanish. Trying to force something to happen only creates a power struggle.

> *There is a story about a captain who was sailing on a battleship and saw a blip on the radar screen that was on their direct course. He quickly sent the message, "Change course 10 degrees south."*
>
> *The message came back, "No, you change course 10 degrees north."*
>
> *The captain radioed back, "I am a captain! Move 10 degrees south!"*
>
> *The reply was, "I am a Seaman First Class, move 10 degrees north!"*
>
> *The captain could not believe the audacity and sent back, "I am a battleship!"*

The answer he received was "I am a lighthouse!"

Have you ever tried to move a lighthouse? The harder I try to force someone to do it "my way", the more they resist and the deeper their heels dig in. Then no one wins. The more you pull on a rubber band, the farther it goes the other way. There is a saying that reads, "He who is convinced against his will is unconvinced still." We can't force others to change.

When we become defensive, we broadcast it to everyone around us. The result is that it brings out the defensiveness in others. Think of what happens when someone angrily yells at you. How do you react? When that happens, we can feel the need to try to protect ourselves in some way.

I remember an incident when my mother had become very critically ill and was in the hospital, unconscious. As I drove to the hospital to be with her, I was immersed in worry and grief. I stopped at a red light, and while waiting for the light to change, just stared off into the distance, not paying attention.

Suddenly, I was startled by the sight of a car crossing directly in front of me, trying to get out of a gas station parking lot. There didn't look like there was enough room for him to get through and I couldn't back up, but he had decided he was going to squeak through anyway. Had I noticed him, I would have stopped farther back to allow him to get out, but in the state I was in, I was not paying attention.

As he drove by my car window, he hurled a very angry comment at me and my first reaction was to get defensive and try to explain to him that I hadn't even seen him. Then I stopped myself and realized that I *should* have been paying attention. I was driving, not daydreaming! I became very grateful to the man for waking me up before something more serious happened.

"Resist not evil" (Mat. 5:39) – the Master Teacher knew that the more we battle with negativity, the more power we give it. The Course in Miracles tells us, "Truth never battles with illusion. Illusions battle only with themselves." When we shine the light of truth on the situation, the need to be defensive disappears. We overcome obstacles, not by resisting them, but by the power of Spirit that is within us.

There is an Aesop's fable that tells the story of the sun and the wind. One day, the wind chal-

lenged the sun to a contest to discover which of them was more powerful.

The wind boasted, "Watch that man below, wearing a cloak. I will blow it right off of him. I am the strongest!" With that, the mighty wind blew and blew and blew. The harder the wind blew, the tighter the man held onto his cloak. Finally, the wind's energy was spent and all became still.

At this point, the sun came out and began to shine. It shone and *shone brighter and brighter, until the temperature rose and the man...... took off his cloak.*

The moral of the story is that gently shining our light is much more effective than blowing our minds.

Lao-Tzu wrote in the Tao Te Ching, "What is, of all things, most yielding can overcome that which is most hard." Imagine a large rock in a fast moving river. Which will wear down first, the rock or the water? The rock. It is heavier and stronger than water and yet, it is the constant resistance against the movement of the water that wears it down.

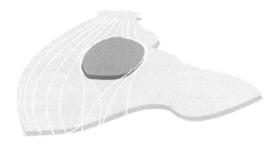

It is like swimming upstream. It is much easier to move with the current. "Going with the flow" can take us on the most amazing, unforgettable journeys.

THE POWER OF NON-RESISTANCE

The fourth characteristic of wholeness is non-resistance, which is the "I of the storm" of defensiveness. It is the contact point between the field of infinite possibilities and the needs of the particular situation, because when we are non-resistant, we allow those infinite possibilities to flow through us.

Living from defenselessness is at the heart of living from wholeness, but to give up being defensive in the presence of a threat is not easy. Something has to change in how we see the situation and what we are making it mean. To "make friends with conflict", we need to understand it.

Change is nature's mechanism of renewal. Without it, we would consist of a planet of newborns. We need change in order to continue to grow. Since everything is in a state of becoming, developing and transforming, then change and movement are the dance of life, the "heartbeat" of the universe. Change is the only way that God can improve things. Despite that truth, whenever there is change or movement, there is the potential for conflict. Here, however, is the important thing to remember. It is not the change that creates conflict. It is the *resistance* to it that causes the difficulty.

The power of "turning the other cheek" as Jesus taught, is that we can literally turn and look at it from a different point of view. We can use our spiritual vision to see it differently. If we stop trying to defend ourselves, if we quit fighting and resisting, then we can embrace the moment and transform any situation into a blessing.

Jesus taught us to "go the extra mile". In those days, a Roman could ask a Jew to carry his cloak. And the Jew had to do it by law for one mile. Jesus said, "Carry it the *extra* mile."

Do you see how difficult this teaching would be for a Jewish person? They hated being forced to do it for *one* mile. What was He teaching? That the first mile was compulsory and the second mile was a freeing choice. Choosing to walk the hero's journey is empowering. That's what He taught! When we stay in a place of love and blessing, we are expressing our true nature. That is the power of it.

For all the fighting and resisting that we do, it is only ourselves that we work against. So it makes sense to allow the flow of Spirit to move through every situation, bringing peace and harmony where there was once discord. The irony, of course, is that the harder we struggle and try to make things happen, the more difficult they are. Richard and Mary-Alice Jafolla tell a story in the book, The Quest, that illustrates this so well.

> *There were armies of land crabs heading to the beach. In order to get there, unfortunately, they had to cross a road. Consequently, driving on that road became very challenging. If the crabs just stayed put, a car could be maneuvered around them fairly easily. The problem was that as a car*

approached, they would rear up as high as they could, which just happened to be the height of a car bumper. This proved to be their downfall.

There were sea gulls on the same road, but they behaved much differently. When a car approached, they didn't challenge or threaten it. They simply got out of the way. They surrendered to the problem and in fact, rose above it.

We can learn to soar above our problems rather than trying to threaten car bumpers. We get in God's way when we resist being present to this moment and our resistance hurts us as much as it does the situation. Ironically, maintaining a gentle, non-resistant posture, and not fighting back, demonstrates real strength. It takes great strength to not lash out at someone who has hurt us.

The famous martial artist, Bruce Lee, said, "Notice that the stiffest tree is most easily cracked, while the bamboo or willow survives by bending with the wind." The tree that moves in the wind and bends with the storms has great power. It is deeply rooted in the earth and yet flexible above the ground. It is that combination of being strongly rooted in truth and yet flexible to move with the storms of our lives that is a measure of our strength.

Through the practice of non-resistance, positive and negative events simply pass by. We don't buy into them. What if all of the experiences of our lives were drawn to us in order to help us grow? Imagine if through those experiences, we had the opportunity to become the avenue through which God showed up in the world? How cool is that!

When we push life away, we are being in the way of God. Imagine being in the way of the universe! Whether we like it or not, we must learn to embrace life completely, without needing it to be a certain way. By doing so, we can discover that who we are cannot possibly be contained by what happens to us. We are not our experience and being present to life means being connected to our experience without pushing it away.

One summer, a few years ago, I went on a white water rafting trip in the mountains of Tennessee. On that trip, I discovered the power of non-resistance. I found myself on a school bus with a couple dozen people, mostly (I noted) teenagers. Every mile that we drove took us closer to our starting point and I saw that the terrain kept getting steeper and the river we were following became more and more turbulent. Hmmm. I wondered what on earth I was doing on that bus, sort of like how you might feel when you are on a roller coaster slowly heading for the top.

Arriving at the beginning point of our journey, at the now *very* turbulent river, I felt some fear and apprehension as I strapped on my life jacket and helmet. The young guide was laughing as she showed us the *proper* way to fall out of the raft. I didn't find it quite as amusing as she did. In fact, I had a little chat with God, right there and then and made it known in no uncertain terms that I did *not* want to fall into that river.

There were 6 of us on the raft. I was given the task of repeating the guide's instructions to the others, since the sound of the rushing water could be deafening at times. At first, I resisted the "job" I had been given, but as time went on, I quite enjoyed shouting to my team members. We began to work together and suddenly, I was loving every minute of being tossed around those rapids.

We came to a relatively calm spot in the water and our guide advised us that if we wanted to get out and experience the current of the river, now was the time. Again, I resisted. But as I watched all of the members of my team plunge, one by one, into the water and head downstream, I dove in.

What a wonderful feeling to relax into the current, lie back in  the sun with my life jacket and just allow the river to pull me along. It made me wonder how many things I have resisted that could pull me through life, and how many times I haven't allowed the strength of Spirit to float me through the daily rapids.

There is a Zen story told of a monk who was journeying to a distant town. In order to reach his destination, he had to follow a rushing river. Suddenly, the banks of the river overflowed and the ground around him swelled with water, pulling him into the rapid current. He struggled and struggled but to no avail.

Finally, he stopped struggling and just let the current pull him along. It deposited him in the center of the town he had been traveling to reach. "Hmm," he thought, "the river brought me here sooner than I would have arrived had I walked."

What tides have you tried to swim against? Being pulled through life by the Power within truly is the pathway to peace.

AWARE-APY QUESTIONS TO PONDER

1. Describe a time when you felt the need to control a person or situation. What happened when you insisted it had to be "your way".

2. How do you react to change?

3. Write about a situation when something changed in your life and you tried to resist it. What happened?

4. Now, "turn the other cheek" and see it from a different perspective. Looking back at this event from where you are now, how has this change been "for you"?

5. Give an example of a time when you "went the extra mile". How did it feel?

CHAPTER 10

TAKING AUTHENTIC ACTION

*Everybody can be great...because anybody can serve.
You don't have to have a college degree to serve....you
only need a heart full of grace, a soul generated by love."
M.L.King Jr.*

THE ENERGY OF BEING AND DOING

Socrates WAS ASKED how to reach Mt. Olympus and he answered, "Just make every step you take go in that direction." Good advice. When our actions are inspired by our spiritual nature, then every step we take leads us in the right direction. Life just gets easier when we follow God's lead. As we have seen, the current of a river moves us forward. We still need to row and steer, but the current takes us on the journey. Following God's guidance and acting upon it can be called "authentic being" and "conscious doing". In other words, being who we came here to be and doing what we came here to do.

During a class in ministerial school, I learned of the four steps to transformation. These are a variation on the four guiding principles of Angeles Arrien. They are: show up, pay attention, tell the truth and respond in love. In other words, be present, stay awake, speak loving words of truth, and take authentic action

What we do in life is connected to who we are and so, being and doing are related. Our soul's purpose is planted deep within us and when we are following Spirit, we are taking authentic action. Imagine for one moment that the entire universe is a giant "university" and you and I are here to take lots of courses. They have names like "How to Shine Your Light 101", "Beginner's Forgiveness" and "Intermediate Self Love" (a pre-requisite before taking "Advanced Love Your Neighbor"). Every day, new lessons appear and we can choose to learn them and move on, or cut classes and then have to repeat! By taking authentic action, we pass the course with flying colors.

Our soul's top priority, in this school, is to help us become aware of all the places where we are not acting out of our wholeness. We can't heal something if we are not aware of it. So, the universe gives us feedback (kind of like a report card), to show us where we are not acting authentically. God needs us to be who we really are!

Where are your actions taking you? Are you moving in God's direction? Are you heading for Mt. Olympus? Do your behaviors match the principles you believe in? As Gregg Levoy writes, "Motion is not necessarily progress, any more than noise is necessarily music." In other words, are we walking the talk? Are we making progress or just a lot of noise? Our behavior is a much better barometer of who we are than the words we speak. Have you ever heard the expression, "After all is said and done, a lot more is said than done."? Our words and actions need to be aligned.

There were five frogs sitting on a log. One decides to jump off. How many are left? Did you answer "four"? Well, there are still five – the frog only decided, he didn't actually jump. The point is that it is not enough just to know about these truth principles. We actually have to practice them - in the School of Life. The Buddha said, "However many holy words you read, however many you speak, what good will they do you if you do not act upon them?" Unity's fifth principle says that when we put these ideas into action, our lives change. Transformation happens as we walk the talk and make sure each step takes us in God's direction.

Without action, we can plan, dream, wish and hope all we want with no results. It is like having a high powered sports car in the driveway, waiting for the key. Authentic action is the difference between *watching* a football game and *playing* in one. Big difference! Life is not a spectator sport. We each have our unique gifts just waiting to be expressed. If who you are is talented, intelligent, worthy, kind and compassionate, then every time you put yourself down or act in a less than loving way, you are not connected, in that moment, with your true wholeness. Conflict can help you gain some insight into those moments. What if everything that happened to us was intended to expose those parts of us that are so afraid? What if, by becoming aware of those frightened parts, we could now heal them, rise to the true Beings that we are, and make the difference in life?

Actions that are not in alignment with who we really are will cause us to be at odds with ourselves. When our actions are based on fear and low self-esteem, we are not moving in the same direction as the Spirit within us, because we are not living out of our authentic self. Failure to act in integrity or speak the truth causes inner conflict. Those actions, rather than authentic are called "unconscious doing" or conditioned behavior. Here is an example of conditioned behavior.

Do you know how they train fleas for the flea circus? They put them into a small box with a glass lid and the fleas soon discover that if they try to jump too high, they hit a "glass ceiling". So they learn to jump only to just below the height of the glass.

The interesting part of this story is that even when the glass lid is

taken away, they still only jump to the height of the glass. They

have accepted an "invisible ceil-
ing" and from that point on, will
never escape from the box even
though there is no longer any-
thing stopping them from leav-
ing!

What "invisible ceilings" have you accepted in your life? What beliefs are you buy-
ing into that are keeping you from being who
you came here to be? What fears are stopping
you from taking authentic action? The important point to remember is that while the head
sees ceilings, the heart knows that the sky's the
limit. Whatever insecurities or fears you may
have, remember, they are not who you are.
When we find ourselves believing in our limi-
tations, then it is time to get back to the heart,
and seek the higher wisdom.

Our heart will tell us the truth -- that the
ceilings are in our minds, that we came here
with a purpose and that we have gifts and talents that no one else has. Our heart will tell us
that we are never too small, too big, too young
or too old to take authentic action and grow
into the spiritual warrior we came here to be.
At the age of 83, the famous architect Frank
Lloyd Wright was asked which of his works he

would select as his greatest masterpiece. He answered, "My next one". No ceilings there.

So, what is your "next one"? What loving action is yours to take? I once heard a Sufi master speak of the power of love. He explained, through a Turkish interpreter, that there are two kinds of love. One kind is what each of us is given at birth. It is like a seed that lies within us, ready to sprout. The other kind is what we allow that seed to grow into. Like a seed in nature, we need to nurture it and feed it in order to see it grow. We do that through authentic action, walking the talk of compassion and service.

> *I read the true story of a man*
> *who was driving on his way to*
> *an important job interview*
> *when he saw a woman stranded*
> *on the side of the highway with*
> *a flat tire. In his mind, he de-*
> *bated about stopping. He was*
> *already late but decided he*
> *would stop and help the woman.*
>
> *He changed her tire and she was*
> *so grateful, she offered him*
> *money for helping her, but he*

waved it off and wished her a good day.

Now he was late for his appointment but decided to go anyway and explain he had been held up in traffic. Upon arriving, he discovered to his surprise that they were running behind schedule and in fact, he was not late at all! "What a blessing!" he thought.

He was unaware of how great a blessing it was, however, until he entered the interview room. There sat the woman in charge of hiring the new employee. Guess who it was? The same woman he had stopped to assist!

Do you think this man got the job? You bet he did! Wouldn't you hire him? By taking authentic action with compassion, he not only blessed this woman, but also blessed himself.

Just imagine for one minute that your actions, right now, on this day, were the pivotal ones that could change your life and in so doing, change the world. Imagine that you have the power to take the step, however small, that moves this planet closer to a place of peace and harmony, where all are honored. Wouldn't you do it? Wouldn't you take that step? That is what our soul desires. It is why we are here!

In the story, The Lord of the Rings, our unlikely band of heroes leaves the comfort of their hobbit home and embarks on a dangerous adventure. Had they seen, in advance, all that they had to face, they would have given up in hopeless despair. Seeing the power of their foe, it appears they are heading for failure and certain death. But by taking authentic action, step by step, they reach victory over that which  seems to be unbeatable.

This "David and Goliath" story is a wonderful illustration of our ability to overcome obstacles that seem insurmountable. As we remember who we came here to be, and act from that remembrance, we can transform any situation. What are your Goliaths? Whatever may be going on in your life, it is there to bring you into a greater understanding of the power within you. What is your David? By that I mean, what "five smooth stones" do you have that can help you to fell the giant? Think about the inner resources that you have. What talents are you blessed with?

Those talents are what God will lead you to use. When our actions are Spirit guided and motivated by who we really are, we can become, as Mother Teresa said, "Pencils in the hand of God, writing love letters to humanity." We become the way of God in action. With God, all things are possible! Jesus taught that truth! Did He say, "*Some* things are possible?" "*Many* things?" " A *few*?" No. He said, "ALL". All things are possible to him or her who believes. Knowing this, we can become, as Norman Vincent Peale wrote, "possibilitarians".

Show up, pay attention, tell the truth and respond in love. When we follow our internal Guidance System, Spirit reveals the way for us to move into action. "Here's a test to see whether your mission on earth is finished," says Richard Bach, "if you're alive, it isn't." So check your pulse and decide if you are ready to become a possibilitarian. Are you ready to transform your life and this planet? In the next chapter, we will learn of a daily practice that will help us to walk the talk and make the difference.

1. What is one "conditioned behavior" that you have that keeps you from experiencing freedom in your life?

2. What is one authentic action you can take to overcome this behavior?

3. Describe an "invisible ceiling" that has kept you from attaining something you want.

4. If this invisible ceiling is your Goliath, what is your David? List the inner resources you have that can help you to overcome this obstacle.

5. Become a "possibilitarian"! On a piece of poster board, make four small signs, reading: SHOW UP, PAY ATTENTION, TELL THE TRUTH, RESPOND IN LOVE. Keep them close at hand, so that you can remember the four rules for transformation. How can you apply these rules to your invisible ceiling?

CHAPTER 11

DAY BY DAY
RECONCILIATION

"Humankind should learn a lesson from the snowflake. No two of them are alike, and yet observe how well they cooperate on major projects, such as tying up traffic".
Anon.

OUR HUMAN FAMILY is meant to work together. As we do, it is inevitable that we may "step on each other's toes" from time to time, and have a need for making amends. We have learned some tools to apply in our every day dealings with others that will help us to use conflict to grow. In the book, "The I of the Storm, Embracing Conflict, Creating Peace", Gary Simmons describes a nightly practice we can adopt to clear up problems as they arise, that he calls "Day by Day Reconciliation". We can use this process to work through things from the past that may be keeping us back.

At the end of the movie, "Harry Potter and the Prisoner of Azkaban", Harry and Hermoine discover that they were successful in a rescue attempt they had made, in part, because the two of them had actually gone back in time, to secretly help themselves out of a jam. How would you like to go on a rescue mission to the past? If you had the opportunity to go back in time and change something that you said or did that was hurtful to someone, what would you choose? Day by Day Reconciliation can have this same kind of "magical effect". By following this practice, we are incorporating the four steps of transformation: Show up, pay attention, tell the truth and respond in love. I will let Gary describe the practice in his own words.

He says, "Several years ago, while closing a metal garage door, I accidentally pinched my fingers in the hinges. During the seconds that followed, amidst excruciating pain, I experienced a total life recall. Similar in many respects to a near-death experience (NDE), my lucid consciousness became preoccupied with memories of moments and circumstances when I failed to live up to my own standards of integrity, when I had inadvertently caused harm or suffering to another. This was polarized by a sense of inner peace, calm and feelings of euphoria. After extracting my ailing hand, I became aware of an urgency to make amends and reconcile myself with those whom I had mistreated or otherwise offended.

"I made a list of individuals to contact or meet and promised myself that reconciliation would be my highest priority. Within a week, I contacted everyone. Much to my surprise, everyone on my list reported that he or she had no animosity toward me and felt that whatever grievance or judgment he or she held was curiously dissolved days prior to my contact."[1]

Gary decided to continue this as a nightly spiritual practice for 21 days. After doing it for three weeks, he had some very interesting results. The practice became easier as time went on, as did creating the nightly list. People who were contacted appreciated it and his relationship with those people was blessed.

During the second week, those on the list reported having *no memory* of the offense having taken place. By the third week, Gary was *instantly* awakened the moment that an event occurred that would have been put on the list. He would stop and relate differently right then, knowing that if he didn't do that, the result would be that he would just have to come back the next day, to revisit the situation. This "reconciliation consciousness" showed up in his

---

[1] Simmons, Gary, The I of the Storm: Embracing Conflict, Creating Peace, Unity House 2001, pg. 152

life as greater harmony, well being and peace of mind. It was a very healing and transformative practice for him and simply through the *desire* for peace and harmony, those things were now showing up in his life.

Using this method of "taking care of unfinished business" each day is conscious doing. It is taking authentic action and walking the talk. If you will commit to following this practice for 21 days, as he did, your life will change. Guaranteed or double your problems back!

In the next few pages, you will find the instructions on how to follow this practice. First, it is necessary to get into a heart centered state before beginning. This is followed by a time of reflection, looking back on the last 24 hours and seeing places where you have not shown up responding in love. The next step is to journal the authentic action you might take in order to resolve the issue. Of course, the fi-

nal step is to follow through the next day on "cleaning up" whatever your heart shows you. Know that you are embarking on a wonderful, healing journey that will bless you and those around you and make the difference in your world.

INSTRUCTIONS FOR
DAY BY DAY RECONCILIATION

BECOME HEART CENTERED

- At the end of the day, at a time when you will be uninterrupted, find a quiet place, sit in a comfortable position and close your eyes.
- Become aware of your breathing and feel your inhalation and exhalation. Don't try to control it, just observe it. With each exhalation, let your body relax and let go of any tension in your body.
- If there are any thoughts, worries or concerns that are weighing on your mind, let them go for now and know that you can pick them up later.
- Feel every part of your body, beginning with your feet, moving up through your legs and hips to the abdomen and back, on to the upper body. Move your aware-

ness to your arms and hands, your shoulders, neck and head. Feel every part of your body. BE HERE NOW.

- Now shift your attention to your heart center and breathe into your heart. Imagine the breath going right into the heart. Become aware of your heart energy as you continue breathing in and out. You may want to place your hand on your heart in order to really feel it.
- Continue breathing into the heart at least 10 times to focus your awareness on your heart
- As you do, think of people, things and situations you appreciate in your life. As each blessing comes into your awareness, feel your heart opening more and more.
- Let the love that is emanating from your heart fill your body.

REFLECTION

- In this state of peace, love and awareness, ask your heart to show you all the instances on this day where you have fallen short of acting from your highest authentic self.
- What was missing for you?

- Had you been more heart centered, how would your experience been different?
- Consider how you would have wanted the situation to turn out.

JOURNALING

- Make a list of two or three situations, as revealed to you by your heart, to revisit first thing in the morning. The objective is to "make right" the situation, now that your heart has shown you a higher way of relating. Make a commitment to reconcile with this person before getting too caught up in the busyness of your day.
- Include any "aha's" and insights that you notice.
- Give thanks for the opportunity that tomorrow will bring – a wonderful gift to free yourself and someone else from the mistakes of the past.

Can you imagine a world where we all followed these practices? Think of the effect it could have in your life. You can be the one that makes the difference in your family, your class in school, your job, your community, your church, your city. Show up, pay attention, tell the truth and respond in love. Remember the snowflakes that stuck together at the beginning of our chapter? Here is a story that shows the power of the individual snowflake. It is by Kurt Kauter, from New Fables.

"Tell me the weight of a snowflake" a coal mouse asked a wild dove.

"Nothing more than nothing" was the answer.

"In that case, I must tell you a marvelous story", the mouse said. "I sat on the branch of a fir tree, close to its trunk, when it began to snow, not heavily, not in a raging blizzard, no, just like a dream, without any violence".

"Since I didn't have anything better to do", continued the mouse, "I counted snowflakes settling on the twigs and needles of my branch. Their number was exactly 3,741,952. When the next snowflake dropped onto the branch – nothing more than

nothing as you say – the branch broke off." Having said that, the coal mouse ran away.

 *The dove, since Noah's time an authority on the matter, thought about the story for a while and finally said to herself, "Perhaps there is only one person's voice lacking for peace to come about in the world."*

Could you be the one?

AWARE-APY QUESTIONS TO PONDER

Commit to practicing Day by Day Reconciliation for 21 days. If you can find a partner to do it with you, then at the end of 21 days, meet with them and discuss what has happened in your life. Send me a description as well: info@imakethedifference.net.

CHAPTER 12

EACH ONE TEACH ONE

"And in the end, the love you take, is equal to the love you make." The Beatles

WE HAVE REACHED the end of our journey together. Of course, our travels have really just begun and it is a journey without end. Let's look back and see the interesting places we have visited.

- We asked ourselves an important question, perhaps **the** most important question we might ever ask -- who have I come here to be? In other words, what gifts have I brought to this planet to share?
- We discovered that every one of us is a unique branch on the same Family Tree. No two alike, each with talents that no one else has in quite the same way. Like a wave of the ocean or a snowflake in a

mountain of snow, we are each an important part of something greater.

- No matter what outer appearances may tell us, the truth is that there is only One Presence and One Power in the Universe, and therefore no one and nothing can be against us.

- When I remember that oneness, it is like the prodigal son returning with great rejoicing and welcome. God is always within us, closer than our very breath, just awaiting our attention.

- Our hearts will lead us on this journey. The intelligence within our heart *knows* who we have come here to be. The heart is the access point through which God connects with us. By loving one another, we open the gates to our own freedom.

- Conflict is a spiritual "midwife" that helps to birth something new. It helps us to grow into something greater.

- People and situations mirror how we are showing up. If we don't feel connected to our sense of wholeness and self worth, then it can feel like life is very much against us, appearing as what we might think of as "the enemy".

- We are in the presence of an "enemy" when we need to be right, need to have things be a certain way, and avoid or re-sist.

- Jesus taught a method of dismantling what looks and feels against us. He said, "Love your enemies, bless them that curse you, do good to them that hate you and pray for them which despitefully use you and persecute you." (Matt. 5:44). These are the Peacemaker's Tools and they are teachings of the heart.

- Judgments are not about us, they may be about what we said or did or what the relationship needs.

- Judgments are *for* us because they show us the places where we are not connected to our sense of wholeness and self worth.

- Listening from the heart and saying "Tell me more" when someone judges us can unwrap the gift that the judgment con-tains.

- We make our lives mean what they mean, by the perceptions that we look through, to view the events that happen to us.

- We can hold those perceptions up to the light of principle and use it as a measur-ing stick by asking, "What am I making this mean?" and "How is it possible that I feel antagonistic when no one and nothing is against me?" or "What spiritual principle supports blame?"

- We may *have* fears and insecurities but they are not who we are. When we act out of those fears, the conflict we experience is from being "who we are not" instead of "who we have come here to be". In order to overcome this kind of behavior, we need to remember to keep in touch with Spirit and live on purpose.
- Being defensive only strengthens our attacker. The real strength lies in non-resistance.
- Following God's lead means walking the talk, taking action and being the one who brings peace to every situation.
- If we love, look and lead with the heart, we are being the way of God instead of in the way.

There are no coincidences in the universe. It is no accident that you have read this book. This is an opportunity for you to live the principles that you came here to demonstrate. Sharing these principles with others can start an "underground spiritual movement" to wholeness that can spread person by person. We can each get in sync with the ever present intention of the universe. That is to be the way, the truth and the life of God. "Each one teach one" simply means taking even one of these ideas and sharing it with someone else. The way to do that is to embody the teaching and live it. *Be it.*

Gandhi was asked what his message for the world was and his answer was, "My life *is* my message." Remember that every word you speak, every action you take is a message about who you are.

Will you live from "who you are not" or will you follow your heart along the path of the Spiritual Warrior and be "who you came here to be". What tee-shirt will you choose to wear? The decision is yours and it is up to you.

I will end this book by quoting Gary Simmons from the end of his book, "The I of the Storm". He says, *"You are called to be a peacemaker as a pathway to God and as a demonstration of your wholeness and worth. The entire universe supports you in making peace wherever you are and in every storm that comes upon you. No one is against you. Make your pathway to God a demonstration of the Truth, for blessed are you who have been called to make peace in a world that longs to know its wholeness and worth. Godspeed!"[2]*

---

[2] Simmons, Gary, The I of the Storm: Embracing Conflict, Creating Peace, Unity House 2001, pg. 155

About the Author

Jane Simmons is an ordained Unity minister and co-director of I Make the Difference Ministries.

A native of Canada, Jane is a former Youth Education Consultant and has worked with children and teenagers for over 20 years. She has facilitated seminars and conferences for spiritual educators.

Prior to leaving Canada, Jane served as the Senior Minister of Christ Church Unity in Hamilton, Ontario and was the Chair of the Canadian Association of Unity Churches.

With a deep interest in holistic health and physical fitness, she is a certified aerobics instructor as well as having a black belt in the martial arts of karate, tae kwon do and jujitsu.

Jane has been a contributor to several publications, including *Unity Magazine, Natural*

Healer Magazine, "Time of Family" Curriculum as well as being published in the book, *New Thought – Practical Steps to Living Your Greater Life*, edited by Rev. Mary Manin Morrissey.

She is the mother of two adult children, and currently resides in Eureka Springs, Arkansas with her husband, Gary. Jane can be contacted at info@imakethedifference.net.